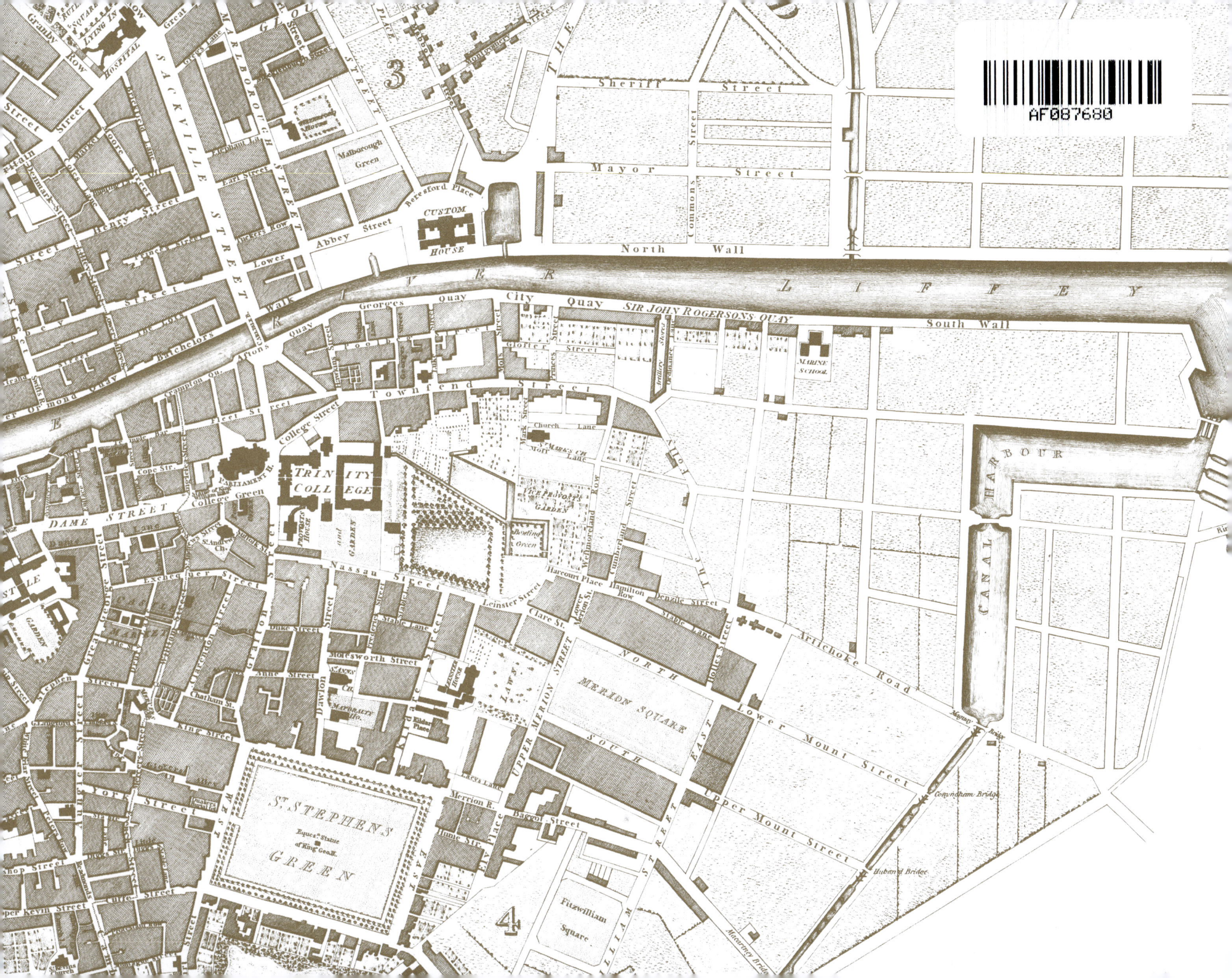

Malton's Views of Dublin

The Story of a Georgian City

Malton's Views of Dublin

The Story of a Georgian City

Trevor White

With **David Dickson, Graham Hickey, Merlo Kelly, Kathryn Milligan** and **Diarmuid Ó Gráda**

Edited by
Djinn von Noorden

MALTON'S VIEWS OF DUBLIN
First published in 2021 by Martello Publishing
Glenshesk House
10 Richview Office Park
Clonskeagh
Dublin D14 V8C4
Republic of Ireland
martellopublishing.ie

Copyright © Trevor White and individual contributors, 2021
Images of Malton's prints reproduced courtesy of The Little Museum of Dublin

ISBN: 978-1-99989-684-3

All rights reserved. The material in this publication is protected by copyright law. Except as may be permitted by law, no part of the material may be reproduced (including by storage in a retrieval system) or transmitted in any form or by any means; adapted; rented or lent without the written permission of the copyright owners. British Library Cataloguing in Publication Data.

A CIP catalogue record for this book is available from the British Library.

Edited by Djinn von Noorden
Book and cover design by Niall McCormack
Printed by Gutenberg Press, Malta
Set in 10pt on 14.5pt Adobe Caslon Pro and Caslon Doric Outline

10 9 8 7 6 5 4 3 2 1

Contents

9 The Great Beauty: Introduction by Diarmuid Ó Gráda

27 A Picturesque and Descriptive View of the City of Dublin: Commentary by Trevor White

85 Best of Times, Worst of Times: David Dickson

91 Picking Through the Details of James Malton's Dublin: Graham Hickey

101 Creating a Route to the Castle: Merlo Kelly

105 A City of Rare Habits: James Malton's Dublin: Kathryn Milligan

110 Note on Contributors

111 Acknowledgements

The Great Beauty
Introduction by **DIARMUID Ó GRÁDA**

EUROPEAN CITIES saw enormous changes during the eighteenth century. Dublin became the second-largest city in these islands, superseded only by London. Relative peace allowed it to spread out. The historic city walls fell into disuse and suburbia gradually emerged. James Malton's views provide striking images of the city during the 1790s when Dublin reached the height of its classical grandeur.

Malton depicted Dublin as one of the splendid European capitals. There are broad thoroughfares lined with elegant buildings and opulent squares of red-brick terraced houses. This is the Georgian Dublin that we cherish today.

When Malton worked in the 1790s, Dublin's role as the premier Irish city was confirmed by its parliamentary function. It was an administrative, industrial and commercial centre, as well as a port. Wealthy merchants were provided with elegant facilities at the Royal Exchange. That grand edifice, ostentatiously placed beside the Castle, found a prominent place in Malton's work. Trinity College, Ireland's only university, doubled its student intake between 1750 and 1800. Malton gave three views of it. Dublin's role as a colonial capital was reflected in the strong presence of the British army. By the 1770s the city barracks held 3,000 infantry and 500 cavalry. Malton gives us a view of the barracks from the south side of the Liffey where the green fields were later filled by the Guinness brewery.

Dublin's social life was dominated by the landed gentry. As early as the 1750s there was enough critical mass to support a lively social scene. This beau monde could be observed in the Castle and at other select venues. Newspapers promoted a wide array of attractions for wealthy people seeking entertainment. Big occasions reflected the scale of the vice-regal court. Up to 1,500 grandees might be seen gathered at the Castle balls.

Owners of country estates spent part of the year mixing with their peers in the city. Malton shows us the monumental town houses of families such as the Kildares, Powerscourts and Charlemonts. Those affluent families encouraged the growth of urban society and their lifestyle had considerable implications for people employed to meet their needs.

Dublin society gained from the English connection. It was part of the circuit for creative artists and

Charlemont House

What Does 'Georgian Dublin' Mean?

Originally a Viking settlement, Dublin was later colonised by the English. The years between 1714 and 1830, when four King Georges reigned on the throne, were a golden age for architecture in the city. The construction of thoroughfares by the Wide Streets Commission, along with a property boom, made Dublin a much grander place – arguably the second city of the British Empire. Architects like James Gandon, Thomas Cooley and Edward Lovett Pearce worked here, and some of our finest public buildings were built during this time.

Many of the builders and craftsmen were Irish, often from Dublin itself.

Henrietta Street, on the north of the city, was one of the earliest Georgian developments. However, society moved south of the Liffey after Leinster House was built for the Earl of Kildare. Townhouses were built around new squares, allowing residents to enjoy lovely gardens in the centre. Merrion Square, St Stephen's Green and Fitzwilliam Square became the most fashionable addresses in Dublin.

entertainers. At the highest level there was an elite network that included the Irish and English capitals. Candidates who failed in the London marriage market might succeed in the 'second city'. Yet Dublin was a very conservative place and insecurity coloured its approach to political controversies. There was a growing uncertainty over many aspects of everyday life.

Dublin's Social Pyramid

As the Enlightenment spread across Western Europe, religious institutions began to lose their influence over everyday life. City councils sought to tidy up the public realm, adding prestige to the property of the power brokers. They created more formal open spaces and strived to keep nuisances out of sight. The grand squares supported a lifestyle based on exclusivity. Parks were reserved for the elite where promenades could yield leisure and sociability.

There were rigid layers in Dublin's social pyramid. The top was occupied by the small elite that controlled everything that mattered. These grandees had houses designed for carriage transport and the best residents were not seen walking the streets. Affluent families often kept their children at home where they were taught by private tutors. Segregation extended to

Malton had several sources of inspiration. This genre of cityscape prints was part of the European tradition of vedute. *It is Piranesi's views of Rome and Canaletto's images of Venice (and London) that are most recalled today. Some were brought back to Ireland by the wealthy sons of the ascendancy who made the Grand Tour of European cultural centres as part of their education.*

household functions and separate stairs allowed servants to enter the house unseen.

A person's outward appearance was a guide to their place in the hierarchy. Wealthy people wore custom-made garments, and wigs, jewellery and perfumes emphasized the good taste of the wearer. Competition between social climbers extended across all the best venues. Within the Protestant churches this contest included purchase of the best seats for Sunday services.

With the rise of bureaucracy and the professions, there was a growing awareness of an emerging middle class. These people were articulate and they were regarded as sober, industrious and thrifty. They brought a new tension to the social structure and their betters made fun of their foibles. Yet they believed they could progress in society on the basis of wealth, regardless of any inherited property, trade or industry.

At the bottom of the social pile were the poor, who passed away a brief existence, seeking food and shelter where they might.

BEHIND THE GREAT BEAUTY

Rapid population growth brought great disparity. Most of the growth followed the influx of poor families from the countryside. There was a very high infant mortality rate and it was the sturdier men and women in their late teens and twenties who were more likely to survive. Even then, they had precarious and miserable lives.

Three decades before James Malton, the renowned artist Hugh Douglas Hamilton compiled an album of street views that were entirely different. Unlike Malton, he concentrated on the gritty facts of street life. His drawings show an elderly blind man with a conspicuous tumour on his nose and a legless man who shunted himself around in a wooden bowl. He included an elderly long-haired man named Joseph Corrigan who was described as the King of the Beggars. Corrigan was confined to a wheelchair and he announced his presence by sounding a horn.

Policing, welfare and health services were operated by parishes of the Church of Ireland. The poorest parishes became dysfunctional and corrupt management marked the entire system. Many parts of the city had atrocious living conditions. Hovels occupied most of the outskirts. Small roadside cottages had a little window on either side of the front door. Low, mud-walled cabins were occupied by paupers.

By the 1770s St Catherine's parish was full of wretched tottering habitations and the laneways off High Street were described as one continuous mass of ruin. Buildings collapsed onto the streets. In Smithfield, fourteen people died in 1783 when a garret floor gave way, together with each successive floor underneath, right down to the cellar. By Malton's time some of the poorest homes in the Liberties were likened to fever hospitals, all occupied by ghost-like wretches.

CHILDREN FOR SALE

Dublin was a dangerous place. Rioting was the most obvious expression of people's grievances. Bystanders were ready to join in and they doled out extreme violence. Housekeepers were encouraged to keep a blunderbuss handy. Gentlemen venturing out after dark were advised to go well-armed. Dublin had its own speciality crimes and robberies attracted most of the death sentences. There were 242 thieves hanged between 1780 and 1795.

Kidnapping was surprisingly common, with victims as young as four years old. Old women lured them with gingerbread, before gagging them and covering them up with a cloak. On one ship the children were found packed into barrels, ready to sail to America. Those kidnappers who were caught were severely punished. One woman stealing three children in Francis Street was killed. Others were thrown into the Liffey, had their ears cut off or were dragged naked through the gutter.

Beggars abducted boys and girls, and they cruelly abused them. A favourite ploy was to disfigure them to arouse compassion in the alms-givers. Limbs might be broken in this process. Some hungry families sold their own children. Destitute mothers in the poorest quarter sold their emaciated boys to chimney sweeps.

Abandoned babies became a feature of street life. Most of them were forsaken by unmarried mothers. During the 1880s the Foundling Hospital took in over 2,000 cast-off children each year, i.e. about six innocents abandoned every day. Children with smallpox were sent to the infirmary and left there to die. Babies with venereal disease were given a tranquilliser that allowed them to die quietly.

The Beaux Walk at St Stephen's Green.

City labourers depended on the vagaries of casual employment. Access to work depended on personal contacts. Rural skills were not wanted and newcomers realized they were not welcome. Migrants fell outside the welfare system, which was parish-based. Many of them kept moving, determined to try their luck in England or America. They were the anonymous poor who occupied a space outside the statistical world.

CASUAL VIOLENCE

Fights with the Ormond Market butchers led to many deaths. Army discipline was cruel and coercive. In 1784 a soldier died after receiving 300 lashes.

There was a casual tolerance of violence. At the pillory the community vented its anger against wrongdoers by pelting them with stones, potatoes and rotten eggs. Offenders endured the pain and the shame of being punished in a public place. Where those sanctions were insufficient the ultimate deterrent was hanging.

Dublin's scaffold was close to St Stephen's Green and it was moved to Newgate in 1783. Executions attracted large crowds. Those being hanged were left slowly suffocating, sometimes struggling for half an hour, surrounded by the shocked groans of onlookers and the distressed cries of relatives and friends.

HUNGER

Poor people occupied the penumbra where it was hard to distinguish between the lowest jobs and mere reliance on charity. It was a grey area marked by all sorts of casual tasks that could put a veneer on begging, whether it was singing ballads, washing down doorsteps or selling kindling for fires. Younger people could try their hand as shoeblacks or link-boys. Street corners and other vantage points were keenly contested and one feature was the prominence of females. Anger and despair could be dangerous emotions when combined with cold and hunger.

Street violence grew and there were periods when the city was running out of control. We see very little of this in Malton's work. His best-known image shows the Beaux Walk at St Stephen's Green. It had already declined when that view appeared. Some change might be suggested by the appearance of two basket-girls, ragged and barefoot, in the background. They are set well away from the refined promenaders.

Beggars wandered all over the city and visitors were surprised by the sheer number of them. Desperate individuals walked down the middle of the street in order to be seen from the houses on either side. Where these tactics brought success, they also brought imitators. In 1769 one woman at Ormond Quay pretended to be mad and tore the clothes off passers-by who refused to give her money. In 1773 the *Hibernian Journal* claimed there were about 2,000 beggars. A decade later the same newspaper estimated the number had grown to 20,000.

WORKERS FIND THEIR VOICE

Guilds – medieval associations of craftsmen or merchants – controlled the manufacture and sale of goods. They regulated working hours and wages. Membership was restricted to males. Most trades operated on a small domestic scale. Employees often lived above the work space, along with their boss. A typical textile unit in the Liberties had about five or six workers. Paper mills, breweries and tanneries spread out along the river banks. By the 1780s Dublin had accumulated about a hundred breweries, distilleries and refineries.

There were several reasons for the decline of the guild system. They were confined to Protestants, and Catholic apprentices were expressly forbidden. Although each master was restricted to two apprentices, this regulation was widely disregarded. Guilds began admitting unqualified individuals – men who were merely looking for the political influence that came with membership.

An added factor was the growth in the size of individual enterprises. Workshops merged into factories and speciality crafts suffered most from mechanization. This weakened the paternalistic structure, especially where money transactions were involved. Such changes had dire consequences for the small workshops that employed weavers and tailors. It was claimed that the Liberties area lost 70 per cent of its plain-cloth weavers during the 1780s. At the same time, new industries such as glass-making were building up larger workforces. Dublin saw an expanding array of shops and by Malton's day, the guilds had lost their monopoly.

Dublin's vice-regal court was a good source of employment for those making quality clothing and provisions. During the constitutional agitation of the 1780s, the Volunteers were encouraged to wear Irish clothes. Unemployed weavers strongly supported these actions and crowded the streets when high society was gathering for Castle balls. Carriages were stopped to check whether the occupants were wearing Irish clothes. During the 1790s the garments of offenders were forcibly removed and destroyed. Tailors using imported

The Parliament House

fabrics were tarred and feathered. Women dressed in English gowns had acid thrown over them and those wearing Spanish shoes had their footwear slashed.

As the guild system weakened, workers' organizations called *combinations* began to emerge. Brute force was used by weavers to secure better terms. As new work practices became more widespread, the aggrieved workers resorted to a violent campaign against innovation. For instance, they broke machines imported from England.

Women and children formed a substantial proportion of the workforce and they laboured under great hardship. Women were excluded from the trades and professions. In Malton's time, one group of unemployed women explained that men had taken a thousand of their jobs and these included tasks as drapers, mercers, milliners, haberdashers, perfumers and toy-sellers. Females arriving from the countryside laboured under two handicaps if they were Catholics and they spoke Irish.

Imports of English cloth put pressure on Irish products and this came at a time when rising prices were already causing great stress to unemployed weavers in the Liberties. It was claimed in 1757 that 20,000 people were suffering from the decline in business. That was a year of near-famine and a fund was set up to assist unemployed weavers. The threat of starvation led some families to the slaughterhouses to collect waste that was normally fed to pigs.

Growing hunger forced redundant workers to search more widely for assistance. Food shops were looted, potato and flour stores were raided and provisions carts were hijacked. The weavers of the Liberties were extremely agitated. Together with their wives they raided bakeries and bacon shops. In 1796 a crowd of over 3,000 people gathered to seize a potato consignment arriving from Waterford.

Crime and Poverty

The criminal code was used to keep poor people in their place. The rule of law became the rule of property. Laws were made to impose sobriety and good sense on the populace. The men of property sought to fix the attention of ordinary people in the workplace. Low wages and high prices could discourage idleness. Across Europe, reformatories were set up to punish the idle poor who refused to work. Dublin had institutions with morally weighted titles such as the House of Correction, the House of Recovery and the House of Industry. Dublin's first workhouse was called the House of Industry. It aimed to get each individual doing useful tasks. Inmates were committed to manual labour in order to pay for their keep. Penitentiaries used solitary confinement and religious instruction to reform the inmates. The houses of correction became penitentiaries promoting a religious awakening. They took in idle paupers whose behaviour upset city dwellers.

The law took a dim view of all the waifs and strays who wandered about the city. They were seen to be uneducated and unprofitable. That made them a threat to society and a burden on the community. Parishes had to do their duty and send them to work for good Protestants. For girls, this form of slavery continued up to the age of twenty-one and for young men it did not end until the age of twenty-four.

Large numbers of mentally-ill people walked the streets. They were cast off and left to die wherever they ended up. When they became an offensive spectacle they were sent to jail where they occupied the darkest corners. Patients in mental hospitals were locked up in cells and heavy iron fetters were used to restrain the more boisterous ones. Out of sight was out of mind and the out-of-mind were out of sight.

As the pressure grew, more institutions were drawn into the welfare system. The parish-based system of social welfare could not cope. They employed whip-beggars to hunt down unlicensed beggars. Down-and-outs stubbornly refused to go and simply turned their begging skills in new directions. They also used their numerical strength and rounded on vulnerable women and elderly men.

Institutions taking in abandoned children were entirely overwhelmed. Youngsters were imprisoned with hardened criminals and orphans appeared with every new episode of war. Soldiers' families ended up begging in the streets. The children of women transportees were taken from them as they boarded ship; these children were left behind, bereft, screaming and crying. The Foundling Hospital ultimately confined admission to the offspring of poor families that could no longer maintain them.

Debtors' prisons were places of predation and they accelerated prisoners into absolute penury. People with means could occupy a suite of rooms while the poorest shared the darkest cubby-hole with a few penniless strangers just as hungry as themselves.

Prisons functioned as holding centres for people awaiting trial. During the 1770s imprisonment came to be regarded as a useful method of punishment in its own right. Managers ran jails as private enterprises, seeing each new arrival as a source of income. Newgate, the city's main custodial centre, occupied a filthy site on the northern periphery. Overcrowding and break-outs were commonplace. In James Malton's time, forty-six prisoners escaped through the sewer.

PROSTITUTION

Diminishing job opportunities drove women into prostitution. Their wailing and screaming expressed an utter desperation. It was always a deadly occupation. Temple Bar was a black spot of the sex trade. Prostitutes were killed by pimps and extortionists. Newborn babies from riverside brothels were suffocated before being thrown into the Liffey, or else dumped in local graveyards and dunghills.

Enterprising prostitutes travelled in carriages fitted with large windows, displaying themselves to potential clients. During the summer months, these market leaders worked the seaside resorts.

Malton revealed the presence of soldiers all over the city and prostitution was blamed for much of the army crime. They broke open the jails to release their favourite prostitutes – in one case the troops set free sixty females from the House of Industry. Army men of all ranks engaged in extortion from the madams, and brothels were ransacked when payment was refused. Barrack Street brothels were the bargain basement of the sex market. Customers traded stolen goods for sexual favours.

It appears that Dublin had more prostitutes per capita than London. Venereal disease was rampant. The Lock Hospital, dedicated to treating VD, was established in 1755. The *Dublin Journal* called for these women to be dispatched to America and the West Indies where white women were urgently needed.

THE DIRT OF DUBLIN

There was scant appreciation of personal hygiene. A bath, even once every few months, was ridiculed as excessive indulgence. The flamboyant beaux were considered eccentric because they insisted on washing themselves every day. Sanitary provision remained very primitive. Many illnesses were attributed to the climate or the local soil: dry, gravelly ground was blamed for tuberculosis while higher ground was blamed for cancer and rheumatism.

Pollution of the water supply became a serious problem. Industrial effluent from brewers, millers, tanners and bleach greens was usually to blame.

Visitors were impressed by the amount of public transport. They thought hackney carriages were more common than in London and the same was said of sedan chairs. Yet hackneys also carried all sorts of dubious loads: they brought convicts to jail and transported infectious patients to the fever hospital. Grave robbers used them to carry corpses.

Domestic sewage was discarded with abandon – poor households simply threw it out onto the pavements. This stinking mess attracted rats and flies. By the 1770s it was widely believed that Dublin had the dirtiest streets in Europe.

Prosperous households emptied their chamber pots into cesspits within the rear yard and relied on private agencies to fill their domestic water tanks. Even in the early nineteenth century a great proportion of the city was still without sewers.

Dunghills drew the most shocking of discarded items. Trinity College adjoined the Townsend Street dunghill and numerous corpses ended up there after being dissected by medical students. A few years before Malton arrived in Dublin, an entire family was found naked and rotting on that dump.

Slaughterhouses were grossly offensive. A mound of animal carcasses blocked the street outside the Newhall Market. The drain running down Cook Street was constantly clogged by gory offal. During the 1770s the Ormond Market was described as a receptacle for blood and guts, giving off an unbearable stink. Local residents threatened to evacuate their houses.

It was hard to find a place to bury the dead. Unlike London or Paris, Dublin retained a sectarian regime of cemeteries. Permission had to be obtained from the Protestant authorities before prayers could be said at Catholic funerals. Graveyards attached to the old churches became heavily overcrowded and the sharp rise in funerals led to the opening of graves that had just been filled. As the Catholic majority grew so did the religious tension.

There was a fear of being bitten by mad dogs. Horses were everywhere and this was made clear by their waste products. Pigs wandered about the city and their aggressive behaviour kept pedestrians at bay. Malton's original painting of the Parliament House showed a swineherd driving his animals along the street but this was left out of the published view.

Insofar as the government had any health policy it was to confine the poorest people to identified quarters so as to contain the spread of epidemics.

Sectarian and Class Tension

Tension in the workplace created a rigid border between rich and poor. Wealthy citizens employed large numbers of servants and this brought the divisions indoors. The female proportion of household servants grew rapidly and new tasks were created for them. Wooden floors, furniture, fittings and ornaments all required maintenance by washing, scrubbing and dusting.

Policing required a sectarian taint. Less than 3 per cent of the city population had a vote and they all comprised rich Protestants. Everyday life was conducted in the streets and markets, and this made the poor more obvious. Sunday gatherings of Catholic workers were considered a threat to public safety. During the late 1770s hurling matches were allegedly drawing up to 10,000 people to the Phoenix Park and the sheriff used great violence to suppress them. Entire crowds were arrested for sabbath-breaking and this heightened the sectarian tension.

There was a distinct class bias in all of this. Popular amusements caused more offence than the genteel ones. Great brutality was used to put down boxing matches and bear-baiting. Poor servants playing pitch-and-toss for halfpennies were hunted down while their employers were close by conducting cockfights and betting fistfuls of shillings, crowns and sovereigns with abandon.

The moral crusade took on a fashionable aspect. Charity sermons in the churches became notable social events, raising considerable funds for city institutions. After 1750 a greater emphasis was placed on the role of wives in creating a domestic haven from the sinful world outside. This improvement programme had a lasting impact. Domestic recreation found favour over public assemblies. Frivolity was confined indoors.

Growing Pains

Dublin had its own high street. It was, however, embedded within the medieval quarter and it fell from grace as the tide of fashion flowed east. The most significant work of the Wide Streets Commission was the formation of a new business district centred on Dame Street, Westmoreland Street and D'Olier Street, reaching across the river into Sackville Street. That is where the new main street emerged.

Better transport facilities gave people greater mobility. The airy squares and broad streets of suburbia proved attractive to affluent residents of the city, while the fashion for sea bathing drew Dubliners out along the bay. Seaside resorts stretched from Ringsend out to Blackrock, and on the north side Clontarf gained an enduring popularity.

Dublin's aristocratic streets became a dwindling proportion of the total. The rest of the city was compared to the London parish of St Giles, where the poorest Irish emigrants had settled.

Yet Dublin's growing pains were not exceptional. A similar pattern could be seen in London and Paris. Ultimately, those people who most needed the support of the community were left behind by those who might be able to help them. ✤

How Do You Make an Aquatint?

DEVELOPED IN FRANCE in the 1760s, aquatint is a printmaking technique that produces tonal effects by using acid to eat into the printing plate creating sunken areas, which hold the ink.

To make an etching, a copper plate is first coated with an acid-resistant bitumen or wax. The etcher scratches through the coating with a fine needle, exposing the bare metal, and then dips the plate into a bath of acid. The lines of the final image are created when the acid eats away or 'bites' the copper. The grooves are then filled with ink. Paper is pressed against the plate, transferring the ink to the paper and creating – that is, printing – an image. The darkness of the printed line depends on the length of time that the plate is immersed in the acid.

Aquatint creates its effect by tone rather than by line. In Malton's time it was commonly used to mimic the appearance of a watercolour painting.

Making an aquatint is a slow and careful process. The base is created by dusting the copper plate with minute particles of resin or asphaltum. The resin adheres to the plate in such a way that when the plate is dipped into acid, the acid bites into the copper around the particles. This results in the ink printing like a watercolour wash.

Degrees of tone are produced by removing the plate from the acid, covering the areas that are designed to print lightly with a coat of varnish, and re-immersing the plate in the acid to allow a deeper 'bite' for darker areas. Malton's prints show at least four tones, particularly in the clouds; his prints were immersed in acid four times. But no fully-coloured prints were published during his lifetime. James Malton's Dublin was black and white. ✤

Key to Map

1. THE UPPER CASTLE YARD, DUBLIN CASTLE – the buildings in the Upper Yard pictured in the View (including the State Apartments on the left, and Bedford Tower on the right) were completed by the mid-eighteenth century.

2. THE PARLIAMENT HOUSE – the south colonnade is pictured, finished in 1729. The building became the Bank of Ireland in 1803.

3. TRINITY COLLEGE, DUBLIN – the West Front including Front Arch, finished in 1759.

4. THE COLLEGE LIBRARY – the Long Room of the Old Library, Trinity College, Dublin, built 1712–32. The high-vaulted ceiling was added in 1857.

5. THE PROVOST'S HOUSE – begun in 1769, fronts onto Grafton Street.

6. ST PATRICK'S CATHEDRAL – founded 1191, with the existing building mainly dating from 1220–59. The church later underwent a full-scale restoration completed in 1865.

7. WEST FRONT OF ST PATRICK'S CATHEDRAL

8. ROYAL EXCHANGE – built in 1769, became City Hall in 1852.

9. THE CUSTOM HOUSE – opened 1791.

10. VIEW OF THE LAW COURTS – better known as the Four Courts, and ultimately finished c. 1802. The building was destroyed in 1922 in the Irish Civil War and rebuilt in 1932. The View is pictured from Ormonde Bridge, destroyed by flood in 1802, with its replacement (now called O'Donovan Rossa Bridge) closer to the building. The old Dublin Bridge in the background was rebuilt in 1818 (now called Father Mathew Bridge). The houses on the south quays were cleared in the early nineteenth century.

11. THE THOLSEL – built in 1676, demolished by c. 1809.

12. THE OLD SOLDIERS' HOSPITAL, KILMAINHAM – begun in 1679. After the dissolution of the hospital in 1927 it eventually became the Irish Museum of Modern Art in 1991.

13. THE ROYAL INFIRMARY – The Royal Military Infirmary, opened in 1788 in Phoenix Park. Owned by the Irish Defence Forces after 1922, and now home to the Office of the Director of Public Prosecutions.

14. BLUE-COAT HOSPITAL – building began in 1773. The tall steeple pictured in the View was never actually completed, with the building's present cupola added in 1894. The building became home to the Law Society of Ireland in 1978.

15. THE LYING-IN HOSPITAL – opened 1757, later more commonly known as the Rotunda Hospital.

16. THE ROTUNDA & NEW ROOMS – the Rotunda was completed in 1764, with the addition of the Assembly Rooms in 1784. The buildings have housed the Gate Theatre since 1930.

17. ST CATHERINE'S CHURCH – current church built 1760–9.

18. THE MARINE SCHOOL – the school moved to this site on Sir John Rogerson's Quay in 1773, moving out in 1872. After use as a warehouse, the building was eventually demolished in 1979.

19. LEINSTER HOUSE – the Earl of Kildare's town house, built 1744. Sold to the Dublin Society in 1814, and eventually became the new home of the Oireachtas (Irish parliament) in 1924.

20. CHARLEMONT HOUSE – built in 1762 for the Earl of Charlemont. Later sold to the Irish Government and eventually became the Municipal Gallery of Modern Art (more commonly known as the Hugh Lane Gallery) in 1931.

21. POWERSCOURT HOUSE – town house for Lord Powerscourt, finished in 1774. After various uses, it became the Powerscourt Shopping Centre in 1981.

22. VIEW OF CAPEL STREET, LOOKING OVER ESSEX BRIDGE – Essex Bridge was opened in 1755, replaced by current Grattan Bridge in 1874. Across the bridge, Parliament Street was finished in 1758, leading to the Royal Exchange.

23. ST STEPHEN'S GREEN – enclosed in 1664, and redesigned into much of the current form in 1880. The statue of George II was blown up by Irish Republicans in 1937. The view is looking from the north-west corner towards the Leeson Street corner.

24. THE BARRACKS – The Royal Barracks, built 1706, became Collins Barracks in 1922 and ultimately part of the National Museum of Ireland in 1997. The fields in the foreground were part of the Guinness brewery and eventually built over.

25. VIEW OF DUBLIN FROM THE MAGAZINE FORT – in Phoenix Park, built c. 1735.

ARMS of the City of DUBLIN.

1. The Upper Castle Yard, Dublin Castle

As the seat of British power in Ireland, Dublin Castle is the obvious starting point for an Englishman's tour of the Irish capital. First built in 1204, the Castle would eventually house the courts, the council chambers, the parliament and a particular frame of mind that blinded itself to Irish suffering.

A fire in 1684 prompted a long rebuilding, and by the 1790s the Castle was 'on the whole, a very respectable pile of Building', according to James Malton, our guide to Georgian Dublin. The first of his Dublin views situates the viewer in the epicentre of the colonial adventure. This is where England plotted to subdue Ireland, and where Malton began his charm offensive.

Unlike many imperial monuments, the Castle remains largely intact, and this plate is the most unchanged of Malton's views, although there are subtle differences in its appearance today. Note, for example, the steeple of St Werburgh's Church in the background of the picture. The tower and spire were later removed on grounds of safety. The building on the right is where the Irish Crown Jewels disappeared in 1907. That unsolved mystery confirmed a long-held suspicion in the Castle: you cannot trust the Irish.

Eventually a peace was made, and on 16 January 1922 Dublin Castle was handed over to the Irish Free State. Michael Collins was seven minutes late for the official handover. He was unrepentant. 'You've kept us waiting 700 years,' he said, 'you can keep your seven minutes.'

Is this picture the first of a series? Or will the artist flake out of a serious commitment? No one has ever produced a group portrait of Dublin in aquatint before. This is a new idea. Yet Malton is clearly influenced by Messrs Cash and Poole. Their 1780 picture book of Dublin features many of the same subjects in the same order. But who remembers them?

In the second half of the eighteenth century the winding, narrow streets of medieval Dublin were swept away as a powerful new body, the Wide Streets Commissioners, reshaped the city. The anti-Catholic Penal Laws were still in force but being relaxed, and Protestant Ireland now had its very own parliament.

Despite the fact that many people lived in conditions of appalling poverty, there was a confluence of political, social and cultural changes, and, in turn, a new confidence. This moment in history has been described as the Golden Age of Dublin.

GREAT COURT YARD, DUBLIN CASTLE.

2. The Parliament House

The first version of this plate has two pigs in the foreground. Beside them are two Dublin hussies (prostitution was rampant in the Dame Street/George's Street area in the mid-1790s).

This commentary on the corrupt inhabitants of the parliament suggests a spirit of iconoclasm, but after reflecting on pigs and prostitutes in parliament, Malton decided to remove them. In the final version of the 'pigs plate', only the dog and the animal-driver remain, and the driver has undergone a rustic makeover. A few acts of mischief aside, James Malton was no rebel.

JAMES MALTON gave us a portrait of the Irish capital that is ubiquitous, but the artist remains an obscure figure. For example, his date of birth is unknown. However, we do know that in December 1765 a James Malton, son of Thomas and Ann Malton, was christened at St Martin's Church in London. This may be our subject.

Thomas Malton was a colonial adventurer of a sort then common throughout the Empire. Based in London, this cabinet-maker and architectural draughtsman was the father of eight children. He was an ideas man and a poor bookkeeper. In 1785 he fled to Dublin to escape his creditors. Here he lectured on perspective and geometry.

In 1769 a competition was held to decide the architect of the Royal Exchange. When the (unsuccessful) designs of James Gandon were published, it may have been Thomas Malton who attacked them in an anonymous pamphlet. Yet he would have had little to gain by savaging Gandon. In fact, he soon asked Gandon to employ his son, James.

James Malton spent three years training as a draughtsman in Gandon's office, while the great master was working on the Custom House. But Malton was sacked because he 'so frequently betrayed all official confidence, and was guilty of so many irregularities'.

The history of Dublin that accompanies these plates is supposedly written by the artist. It claims that 'confining ourselves only to the part [of the parliament building] exhibited in the annexed View, is … the noblest structure Dublin has to boast'. Malton focused on his favourite part of the building, built by Edward Lovett Pearce, rather than the more recent curved additions to the east and west. After Pearce's death, James Gandon built a new entrance at the east of the building.

In 1793, when this etching was first published, you would have seen a fine equestrian statue of King William III, just out of frame to the left. Today the view is obscured by London plane trees.

THE PARLIAMENT HOUSE – DUBLIN

3. Trinity College, Dublin

People were shorter back then; note the low railings outside the college. They were replaced by loftier railings.

In 1791, at the age of twenty-six, James Malton finished his preparatory drawings for a group portrait in aquatint titled *A Picturesque and Descriptive View of the City of Dublin*. Today these twenty-five plates are known as *Malton's Dublin Views*. Not exactly a book, nor simply a collection of pictures, Malton gave the world a large, coffee-table tome with luxurious production values, handsome bursts of text and spruced-up renderings of architectural gems. These extraordinary prints are the bare bones of a great Dublin drawing room.

Malton's renderings are over-polished in a way that flatters Dublin, often concealing the reality of life in the city. (If he were working today, it is inconceivable that a tram would disturb the splendour of this vista.) The artist's benign gaze partly explains the allure of the work. Maurice Craig said Malton's ability to 'convey an atmosphere of Arcadian clarity' is one of the reasons why his work remains so popular. That phrase 'Arcadian clarity' is not exactly a compliment. It could be used to describe the John Hinde postcards of Dublin in the 1960s.

The truth is that Georgian Dublin was an elegant kip. Even at the height of its fame, public drunkenness was a daily spectacle, and many people lived in squalor. An English actor called Samuel Foote once said he didn't know what the beggars of London did with their old clothes until he saw the beggars of Dublin. But look – where are all the mendicants in this image?

Malton's decision to sanitize street life was typical. His brother Thomas did the same thing in his surveys of Oxford and London. It was the commercial thing to do. As for his subject: Trinity College is the oldest seat of learning in Ireland. In the eighteenth century it became an exemplar of classical public architecture. And, as usual, Malton is in the right place at the right time, depicting Trinity in all its finery. There is no better guide to Georgian Dublin on a sunny morning, except that those blue skies were added later, fifteen years after he died, by another artist. The weather changes in every hand.

TRINITY COLLEGE, DUBLIN.

London, Published March 1st 1793, by Jas. Malton.

4. The College Library

JAMES MALTON never studied in the Trinity College Library. He had little formal education. In 1786 an author called Publius mentions a 'young artist' who had been a drawing clerk in the office of James Gandon since the age of seventeen. We now know that James Malton was dismissed by Gandon after only three years because he couldn't keep his mouth shut. In 1787 he is said to have written an anonymous attack on Gandon in a book called *Letters to Parliament*. Outrage and family loyalty would later inform the young man's depiction of Dublin's great buildings. Bad blood with an old boss coloured the whole endeavour.

Despite being sacked by Gandon, James Malton refused to leave Dublin for good. After trying and failing to become the head of architectural drawing at the Dublin Society, he published his first architectural studies, unremarkable views of Heywood Demesne and Castle Durrow, in 1789. Then he embarked on a thunderclap project to advertise Dublin to itself and the world.

Malton dedicates his fourth plate to Edmund Burke, a graduate of Trinity. Now regarded as the father of conservatism, Burke was born in Dublin but lived most of his life in London – he made the opposite journey to Malton – and was a brilliantly original critic of his age. This salute from an artist to a statesman is perhaps the most touching fragment of autobiography in all the views.

Yet we know little about Malton, the Englishman who gave us the definitive portrait of Georgian Dublin. Many art critics regard his work with disdain, and while it is often displayed, the work is seldom subject to scrutiny. His œuvre is too commercial or generic to be considered with any delicacy. Burke becomes a giant in death, while Malton sinks into relative obscurity. We don't even know what he looked like.

In 2018 a million people came to this library to view the Book of Kells. It is arguable that Ireland's greatest cultural treasure has no real connection to Dublin – mind you, neither did James Malton.

COLLEGE LIBRARY, DUBLIN.

London. Pub.d by Jas. Malton & G. Cowen, Dublin. July 1793.

5. The Provost's House

MANY MANSIONS, squares and terraces were built in the second half of the eighteenth century, turning the dank town of Dublin into one of the finest capitals in Europe. This house at 1 Grafton Street is a good example of the city's new grandeur. It was built in 1759, the year Arthur Guinness started to brew stout. Designed for the Provost of Trinity College, the house boasts a Palladian facade inspired by Lord Burlington's house in London. Malton describes it as 'the second [greatest] private Structure in Dublin'.*

In this plate, the dome of what was then the Chapel rises over the buildings of Library Square. By 1791, however, the tower and dome had become unsafe and were taken down. Malton probably sketched his reference for this print while the dome was still standing, although the plate was not released until 1794.

The Provost's House is less visible from the street today. The only large eighteenth-century townhouse in Dublin that remains a private residence, it is still home to the Provost.

* The grandest residence in town was Leinster House, to which the artist would shortly turn his attention.

Coppinger Row. Capel Street. Grafton Street. Look out for the street signs in Malton's Dublin. They lend the project a veneer of stolid veracity.

The Georgian era includes most of the eighteenth century and the early decades of the nineteenth century. Today, Georgian Dublin constitutes less than 5 per cent of the city, but still informs our image of the capital.

PROVOST'S HOUSE, DUBLIN.

6. St Patrick's Cathedral

WELCOME TO THE southern limit of Malton's Dublin. Founded in 1191, St Patrick's Cathedral is the National Cathedral of the Church of Ireland. If you were important and rich, this is where you spent your Sunday mornings. Even in Malton's time it was synonymous with Jonathan Swift, our greatest satirist, who was Dean of the Cathedral until his death in 1745. Four years later, architect George Semple added the spire. At forty-three metres in height, it made St Patrick's the tallest church in Ireland.

You are not looking at an architectural masterpiece. Malton complains of the Cathedral that 'being built in a hollow, […] this keeps it very damp and dirty, and is bringing it quickly to ruin'. In the immediate foreground a man and his dog recline on a tombstone.

Malton references a fire at the copperplate printer's that destroyed two of the plates, delaying publication and forcing him to find an alternative printer. This is one of two plates that were probably destroyed by fire.

This view shows the Cathedral before the nineteenth-century restorations, including the rebuilding of the Lady Chapel (on the right) in the 1840s, and the lavish attentions of Sir Benjamin Guinness some twenty years later. Beer and the church – a stout arrangement.

In the early 1800s the population of Ireland was about six million. There were twelve million people in England. For the British, Ireland was a difficult, often unruly part of the Empire and a potential threat across a short stretch of sea. The Act of Union, which forcibly incorporated Ireland into the United Kingdom of Great Britain and Ireland, left Dublin politically castrated.

SAINT PATRICK'S CATHEDRAL, DUBLIN.

London, Published March 1st 1793 by Jas. Malton.

7. West Front of St Patrick's Cathedral

IN MALTON'S WORK, some tantalizing glimpses of the early Georgian city slip through, such as the ranks of 'Dutch Billy' gable-fronted houses beside St Patrick's Cathedral – as well as an early pan-tiled roof in the foreground. Note the man under the 'Cross Poddle' sign. Originally a crossing point for the River Poddle, this very short street (now called Dean Street) contains all the history of Dublin.

The River Poddle rises in the Cookstown area north of Tallaght and is today culverted, though it still runs under Dublin Castle. The Castle, built when the River Liffey was much wider, was once effectively defended by both rivers. At low tide you can still see the confluence of the Poddle and the Liffey near the Clarence Hotel on Wellington Quay.

Malton was one of the first generation of artists to exploit the aquatint process and engraved his own plates. Well able to draw his own human figures, it has been said that he may have employed other artists such as Robert Smirke and Francis Wheatley to reveal Dublin's colourful citizenry. But we all cut corners on occasion. In the *Dictionary of Irish Biography*, Daniel Beaumont offers this description of Malton: 'a brilliant draughtsman and a master of perspective but his views cannot be taken at face value; on occasions he altered the dimensions of buildings (or even added details that were not actually there in the 1790s) so that they would make better compositions'.

The Dutch Billy houses in the background have now been replaced by a park.

WEST FRONT of St PATRICK'S CATHEDRAL

8. ROYAL EXCHANGE

THE WIDE STREETS COMMISSION was a forerunner to the modern city council. Its first act was to create Parliament Street, an avenue from Capel Street Bridge to Dublin Castle.* This produced a 100-square-foot site dominating the approach to the bridge – a good location for the new Royal Exchange. One of the first great buildings in the neoclassical style, it would be the commercial centre of Dublin.

In 1852, after what Maurice Craig called 'various vicissitudes', this building was renamed City Hall, becoming the home of Dublin's City Council. Today it is where one might secure more residents' parking, the erection of a zebra crossing or the beginning of a political career. (Incidentally, have you ever noticed that Dublin's City Hall is located on Cork Hill?)

Ceremonies are often conducted downstairs in the great hall, despite the terrible acoustics. The design was intentional. If you walk around the outer ring of the Rotunda you will hear a distinct reverberation. Cooley designed the building to create an echo that would muffle any conversations had while strolling around the room. Power requires privacy.

Diarmuid Ó Gráda writes that the Wide Streets Commissioners wanted strict unity in the public realm. 'In Dame Street, there was a ban on any windows or advertising signs projecting to the front of the buildings.' It is not simply nostalgic to neglect the demise of that statute.

The Royal Exchange was where you exchanged your Irish pound into English sterling. James Malton calls it 'one of the principal ornaments of the City, from the combined advantages of an excellent Situation, beautiful Form, and fine display of architectural elegance'.

ROYAL EXCHANGE, DUBLIN.

9. The Custom House

MALTON WAS LOOKING down the river in this view of the Custom House. The vista was later corrupted by the erection of the Loopline Bridge. In 1790 Malton published a different print of the same building, along with an early version of the Parliament House, as though to test the market. Would anyone buy these images of Dublin?

James Gandon's first large-scale commission in Dublin, the Custom House, was designed in 1781 and would have been finished by the time this plate was published. However, by that point, Malton was on foul terms with Gandon. As a result, this work contains a blunder.

There were 'soup-tureen' urns on the corner pavilions of the building. In Malton's picture they are absent. The omission was, wrote Craig, 'a clear indication that Malton was still, by 1799, on such bad terms with Gandon that he could not do as artists normally did with unfinished buildings: procure drawings from the architect and work from them'.

In the accompanying text, Malton does not forget to applaud the architect: 'It was designed by, and executed under the direction of Mr. James Gandon; the objections made to it by the interested or the ignorant are now forgotten, and it will, we trust, long continue a magnificent monument of the genius of that able architect.' This praise seems strange, given what we know about the relationship between the artist and the architect, his former employer. What was Malton trying to do here? Did he want to impress Gandon? Or was he the real author of the text?

We know that Malton employed artists to 'help finish' his work. For example, the engraved script on the title page of his *Dublin Views* is by another hand. But Malton remains something of a mystery. Experts don't know what inspired him to produce his views. Even Andrew Bonar Law is stumped: 'As he was trained as an architect and draughtsman, one cannot help wondering why he digressed from his main calling into the production of what might be called a "coffee-table" book. Perhaps he wished to prove himself to Dublin society.'

In 1780 a decision was made to relocate the Custom House to its present position east of O'Connell Street (then Sackville Street). It was without doubt of strategic interest to many members of the Wide Streets Commission, such as Gardiner and Fitzwilliam, who were developing their estates to the east of the city. Designed by James Gandon, the Custom House was officially opened on 7 November 1791 at a cost of £200,000.

CUSTOM HOUSE, DUBLIN.

London Publish'd July 1792 by Jas. Malton and G. Cowen, Dublin.

10. View of the Law Courts

This has traditionally been the third most popular plate in the series, 'because all lawyers are rich,' according to Andrew Bonar Law. It was one of the last plates to be completed. We know this because the Four Courts were still unfinished at the time of the Act of Union in 1800. After the creation of his source drawings for the views in 1791, Malton went back to London, but he returned to Dublin periodically to check on changes to the buildings before particular etchings, such as this one, were printed.

Construction of the Four Courts began in 1776 from the designs of Thomas Cooley, but after the architect's early death, James Gandon was appointed to finish the building. The feud between Gandon and Malton is immortalized in the artist's mistakes. For example, he incorrectly depicts the ground-floor front-of-wing windows as round-headed rather than square-headed. More seriously, he fails to convey the grandeur of the dome yet criticizes Gandon for deviating from the plans of the original architect, lamenting 'that idea has been departed from by [Cooley's] successor, a change, which, besides other disadvantages, prevents so magnificent a structure being seen to advantage'.

When in Dublin James probably stayed with his father Thomas and brother Thomas Junior, who was also an architectural draughtsman. The Malton family tree is complicated by the fact that Thomas Junior also trained under Gandon. Sibling rivalry remains a powerful drug. Was James inspired by, or determined to outdo, his older brother? A successful artist whose survey of London boasted a hundred aquatint prints, Thomas was widely admired in his day although James is the more enduring presence.

The Four Courts were almost completely demolished during the Irish Civil War, with the loss of priceless legal and historical records. A century after this act of mass vandalism, a groundbreaking project is underway to digitally recreate the contents of the Public Records Office.

VIEW OF THE LAW-COURTS, LOOKING UP THE LIFFEY. DUBLIN.

11. The Tholsel

Here is the Malton 'atmosphere of Arcadian clarity' at its most hygienic, in a Dublin devoid of dogs, dirt and horse manure. *Look! there are no pigs foraging in sewers and dunghills.* The Tholsel was demolished at the end of the 1780s. This handsome edifice, at once familiar and remote, is central to our understanding of early Georgian Dublin. As usual, Malton gets the goods in the nick of time.

The building is long gone and there is nothing familiar about the view. As a result, this was long the cheapest plate, and it is still known in the trade as the wedding print. If you had to get your uppity Dublin cousin a present for her big day, you might buy the Tholsel. Some brides have several copies. In this way, it manages to be popular and unpopular at the same time.

The first Tholsel was built in the fourteenth century, but the one pictured here, on Skinner's Row near Christ Church Cathedral, dates to 1676. The name means 'toll-gatherer's stall'. Serving as meeting chamber and exchange, the Tholsel had a timekeeping function, with its large public clock, and was synonymous with law and order. Criminals were 'whipped at a cart's tail from the Tholsel to the Parliament House'. And it was here Dubliners came to watch the burning of libellous publications, gaming tables and fraudulent goods. In 1718 the sum of £1,000 was offered to anyone who could name the person who broke into the Tholsel and defaced the portrait of George I. The culprit remains unknown.

The Tholsel has not completely disappeared. In the crypt of Christ Church Cathedral, the statues that once adorned it are still on public display, along with the Royal Coat of Arms. These lonely idols, hidden underground, remind us of what was once a great centre of civic life.

THOLSEL, DUBLIN.

12. The Old Soldiers' Hospital, Kilmainham

A CRITIC ONCE NOTED that Ireland's leading contemporary art collection is housed in 'the remote Tibetan fastness of Kilmainham'. While the location is obscure, and some of the galleries a bit pokey, visitors are well advised to make the journey, for this is the oldest classical building in Ireland. Construction started in 1679. When it was envisaged as a home for injured or infirm soldiers, along the lines of Les Invalides in Paris, Malton calls it 'the Old Man's Hospital'. Some of the earliest residents were wounded at the Battle of the Boyne.

Now known as the Royal Hospital, it was handed over to the Free State in 1922. Five years later, the last pensioner was moved to its sister institution, the Royal Hospital Chelsea in London. The hospital was dissolved in 1927 and for twenty years the building served as the headquarters of the Garda Síochána. It then fell into disrepair and lay vacant until the 1980s, at which point Taoiseach Charles Haughey decided to renovate it at a cost of three million punts. To give him credit, Haughey recognized the value of our architectural heritage at a time when most government ministers did not have a cultural bone in their bodies.

It took four years to restore the hospital – the same length of time it took to build it three centuries before – and since 1991, it has been home to the Irish Museum of Modern Art (IMMA). Ireland's oldest classical building is now one of our greatest museums. Malton would surely approve.

The gardens on the left edge of this print were originally used for medicinal purposes, but over time they became the private gardens of the hospital Master.

The building encloses a square courtyard with arcaded walks, over which are corridors that allow access to the wards. The northwest corner, on the right in the plate, housed the master of the hospital, then General Cunninghame, Commander-in-Chief of the British forces in Ireland and the dedicatee of Malton's print.

OLD SOLDIERS HOSPITAL, KILMAINHAM, DUBLIN.

13. The Royal Infirmary

Apart from the Tholsel, this building – designed for sick and wounded soldiers – is the least well-known of all Malton's subjects. But unlike the Tholsel, it still stands. The Office of the Director of Public Prosecutions now occupies the Infirmary.

THE GOTHIC NOVELIST Charles Robert Maturin wrote of his Dublin: 'Its beauty continues [...] but it is the frightful lifeless beauty of a corpse, and the magnificent architecture of its public buildings seems like the skeleton of some gigantic frame, which the departing spirit has deserted: like the vast structure of the bones of the Behemoth, which has ceased to live for ages and around whose remains modern gazers fearfully creep and stare.'

Maturin was given to sublime exaggeration. Malton was more pragmatic. In his notes for this plate, he compliments the placement of the Royal Infirmary ('delightfully situated … commanding extensive and uninterrupted prospects over the [Phoenix] Park') but neglects to mention that the building was designed by James Gandon. Maybe quite enough damage had been done to the relationship between the two men by this stage. Or is the omission a further slight?

Posterity was certainly a factor. Malton designed these views for the benefit of an exclusive audience. In that regard his six-quid survey of Dublin's architectural wonders is a grandfather to deluxe, creative magazines like *McSweeney's* or *Visionaire*; an entrepreneurial but slightly worthy attempt to move the market along by giving Dublin a facelift. In the engraver's mind, it was a commercial endeavour as much as an artistic achievement. This plate, for instance, is dedicated to the commissioners of the Royal Infirmary. Would *you* buy a picture that was dedicated to you?

James Malton hoped the answer was yes.

ROYAL INFIRMARY, PHOENIX PARK, DUBLIN.

14. Blue-Coat Hospital

NONE OF THE GREATEST architects from Georgian Dublin was from Dublin. 'Thomas Ivory of Cork' was at least Irish. Malton pays a misinformed homage to him in this lively, well-dressed scene. Outside the Blue-Coat Hospital we see a mother and her children; soldiers on parade; and, crucially, a tower over the central entrance that was never actually built. The fantasy steeple gives the game away. Now we know that Malton constructed his view from Ivory's architectural plans. This is not a life drawing at all.

Ivory won a competition to design this building, but the project's ambition was greater than its budget. By 1779, as the main block neared completion, it was decided that the hospital would not receive a large quadrangle to the rear. Ivory resigned in disgust. His graceful tower was never completed beyond a stub, and even this stub was eventually removed in 1894. The cupola visible today is a later addition.

Unconcerned by Ivory's decision, James Malton praised the 'very happy effect' of the architecture, 'which fails not at once to strike and interest the beholder'. (He was an early publisher of single-sheet advertisements.) In reading the notes that accompany each plate, a pattern is now clear. We are offered a long, sickly-sweet description of each location, complete with dedication to patrons potential or real.

The whole endeavour feels overtly public, as if the artist is trying to seduce the ruling elite and anyone else who will swallow his outrageous blandishments.

The King's Hospital and Free School was founded in 1669. The school opened in 1674, moving to the site pictured when it was finished in 1783. It was more commonly known as the Blue-Coat School or Hospital. The school eventually relocated to Palmerston in 1970, and the Law Society of Ireland moved into the building in 1978.

BLUE-COAT HOSPITAL DUBLIN.

London, published March 1798, by Ja.^s Malton.

15. The Lying-In Hospital

This is the scene outside the Rotunda, founded as the Lying-In Hospital 'for the relief of pregnant poor women'. Note the man begging on the bottom right: hand out, cap open. In 1783 the *Hibernian Journal* lamented, 'Humanity must shudder at the crowds of petitioning wretches to be met in every corner of the city.' Seven years later James Malton decided to ignore the reality of begging in Dublin. His Cavendish Row and Parnell Square are largely spotless, with well-to-do people on foot and in carriages. Here is a lone, subversive presence.

The Rotunda is the oldest continuously-operating maternity hospital in the world. The main block resembles Leinster House, another of Malton's subjects. Both were the work of the same man, German architect Richard Cassels (or Castle). Malton gives the view a sterile gloss, but at first the building was so badly ventilated, and disease so rampant, that one out of six babies died in its first nine days.

The hospital is distinguished by its cupola. The curved, colonnaded wings on either side originally ended in simpler pavilions, but Gandon replaced them with more elaborate ones in 1784. These include his characteristic triumphal arches, inset columns and decorative urns. They look fantastic.

If Malton wanted to challenge Gandon's reputation, this project was a poor idea. Two centuries after the fact, these plates celebrate Gandon's hand in Dublin. What do we not know about a relationship that was almost certainly deeper and more complex than we imagine? Was Malton a Boswell figure to Gandon, perhaps? Or was it a master–servant relationship? What is going on here?

Diarmuid Ó Gráda reminds us that the top of Dublin's social pyramid was occupied by 'a small elite that controlled everything that mattered'. This boisterous, lively, glittering society flourished until the Act of Union saw Dublin cede authority to London, and with it the wealthiest lords of the land.

LYING-IN HOSPITAL, DUBLIN.

London. Publish'd Dec.r 1795.

16. The Rotunda & New Rooms

THIS VIEW IS FULL of historical baggage. You may have to adjust your eyes. At the front you see the Ambassador Theatre, which is now home to exhibitions about dinosaurs, large animals and human bodies. Beside it is the Rotunda Annex, which is now the Gate Theatre. You can also see the Rotunda Gardens in the background. The whole is familiar and strange.

Maurice Craig describes the Rotunda as the centre of a 'constellation of pleasure-rooms which brought in an income to support the hospital'. Malton writes that the Rotunda had 'a grand effect on public nights' when 'filled with the native beauty and fashion of the country'. Its fundraising soirées were popular, although the organizers were criticized for holding concerts on a Sunday evening, thus violating the Sabbath.

The views were a decade in the making, but Malton spent most of that time in London. By 1792 he was living in Soho. Many of his Dublin studies were exhibited at the Royal Academy and finally, after six parts were published individually, the whole collection of twenty-five aquatints was published in a single bound volume. In 2018 a framed set sold at auction for €12,000.

Malton's Dublin is full of strange afterlives. The Gate Theatre was founded in 1928 by Hilton Edwards and Micheál MacLiammóir. Famous for producing experimental European theatre, it was described as Sodom to the Abbey's Begorrah. Orson Welles started his career in this great Dublin institution.

Designed by John Ensor and built in 1764, the Rotunda was initially a simple brick building but the many additions evident in this plate were made in 1784.

ROTUNDA & NEW ROOMS, DUBLIN.

17. St Catherine's Church

Some of Malton's thoroughfares seem abnormally quiet, while others are shown with very light traffic and a few unhurried pedestrians. Here, St Catherine's Church sits stoically, almost marooned, about the brick vernacular of the ancient highway to the agricultural hinterland. Perhaps the artist did his fieldwork early in the morning or at other quiet times. What is certain is that he was no social realist. Rather, he decided to sanitize Dublin. So here is St Catherine's Church on Thomas Street on a fine day, with a few Dubliners milling about. As usual, the streets are spotless and the sky is quite clear. This is art as press release.

Why is Malton such an enduring presence? Although he was, in David Dickson's phrase, 'a quite exceptional draughtsman', there was nothing unique about his style. Perhaps we admire his determination to show off the city to the world. Desperate for external validation, we acknowledge the benign presence of an Englishman who flatters Dublin and suggests, even, that the city is worthy of her august reputation at that precise moment.

Malton is not alone in making a star of Dublin. His equivalents in the field of photography include Charles Cushman (1896–1972) and Evelyn Hofer (1922–2009). One was American, the other German-American. Outsiders seem to appreciate the city in all its shabby glory; there is less of the provisional affection that many locals have about 'dear dirty Dublin'.

St Catherine's is, of course, a sacred site in Irish nationalism. The patriot Robert Emmet was hanged in front of it for high treason on 20 September 1803. Malton died two months earlier. He had no idea that St Catherine's would soon become central to Irish republicanism.

Malton was an accidental historian. He dates the church to 1105. In fact, it was originally built in 1185. Like several churches in Dublin, St Catherine's never received the tower that was intended and still has the stunted appearance of Malton's plate.

St. CATHARINE'S CHURCH, THOMAS STREET, DUBLIN.

18. Marine School

IN THE 1690s a ship called the *Ouzel Galley* left Dublin for the Ottoman port of Smyrna (now Izmir in Turkey). The galley was due to return the following year. But the *Ouzel* would not come home that year, nor the year after. After three years, Dubliners assumed she had been lost at sea along with her crew. Wives remarried; estates were divided amongst next of kin.

Many years after she had left Dublin,* the *Ouzel* sailed back up the River Liffey, her hold full to bursting with pirate booty. The captain claimed that the ship fell victim to Algerian corsairs, who forced them to engage in acts of piracy. After years in captivity, the captain and his men managed to retake the *Ouzel* and sail home. Was the mission to Smyrna a front all along? And was it the captain who led his crew in piracy? No one really knows. But the *Ouzel Galley* is still remembered in Hiberno-English, and in certain parts of Dublin; illegitimate children from Ringsend were once known as 'Ouzelers'.

The Marine School is one of two Malton subjects that no longer exist. Generations of seamen learned their trade in the school, on the left side of the print, on what is the south bank, looking up the Liffey. Gandon's Custom House is visible, even conspicuous, on the right.

Malton boasts that the school is 'seldom so distinctly seen as in the annexed View, the Shipping in the harbour and about the dock crowdedly intervening'. But the print offers a better view of the river than the school. Like an ardent lover, he saw no harm in exaggerating the virtues of Dublin.

* *Estimates vary. We are in the realm of Dublin legend.*

Malton notes that the Marine School was 'built as a Nursery for Orphans, and unprovided Sons of Seafaring Men'; in effect it provided a free education for the sons of seafarers who had lost their lives or suffered disabilities at sea.

MARINE SCHOOL, DUBLIN, LOOKING UP THE LIFFEY.

London, Publish'd June 1796, by Jas. Malton.

19. Leinster House

The most impressive architecture in Georgian Dublin was north of the River Liffey until 1745, when the Earl of Kildare decided to build this great house on the south side. The axial placing of the house meant it dominated Molesworth Street as it would later come to dominate Merrion Square. Dublin would never be the same again. The earl's decision to build a country-style mansion on the edge of town, on what was then called Molesworth Fields, was rather cunning. 'Wherever I go,' he boasted, 'fashion will follow me.' He was right.

After the Act of Union, the duke remained in Dublin for a decade, but Leinster House was eventually sold to the Dublin Society (now the Royal Dublin Society). It was their headquarters for over a century, and two wings were added on either side. We know them as the National Library and the National Museum. Imagine if this jewel of a plaza were open to the people of Ireland, without a big gate and iron railings.

Leinster House has been the seat of the Irish parliament since the foundation of the State. In 1963 US President John F. Kennedy reminded the Dáil that the original inhabitant said it 'does not inspire the brightest ideas'. Malton was an early casualty of this phenomenon, or else the woman on the first floor balcony is levitating – there is in fact no floor for her to stand on beside that window.

Leinster House was thought to be a model for the White House in Washington DC. Its Irish architect, James Hoban (1758–1831), was introduced to the mansion when the Earl of Kildare became the Duke of Leinster in 1776, the same year America declared its independence from Britain.

LEINSTER HOUSE, DUBLIN.

London, Publish'd July 1792 by Jas. Malton and G. Cowen, Grafton Street, Dublin.

20. Charlemont House

In James Malton's time, Dublin was the show-off capital of English rule in Ireland. But in the last five years of his life there were two rebellions in Dublin, and in 1801 the country lost its parliament. He went down with the old dispensation.

Here is what we now call the Hugh Lane Gallery. The streets are spotless and the sun is shining, but not too much; well-dressed people and a dog populate the scene but do not crowd it. (There are many canines in Malton's Dublin; mostly it's the same small dog on its hind legs. Perhaps this is the artist's much-loved pet?) Malton seems afraid of corrupting his own architectural and social idiom.

These pictures are an advertorial for the architectural metamorphosis of the second city in the British Empire. The sun-drenched streetscapes depict the colour of Dublin, its grand public buildings and a string of set-piece vistas. The effect is scintillating and timeless; even today, it still represents an ideal Dublin. With better health and better marketing the artist might have lived to enjoy his own success.

The elite would later distance itself from the dregs of Dublin by repairing to the new suburbs. By 1834 you could get into town on the train. And this continued after independence, as Desmond Guinness observed: 'When Dublin became a capital once more, there was a chance that some of the great townhouses might have come to life again as foreign embassies, but most of those had moved out to Ballsbridge, a Victorian suburb reminiscent of North Oxford.'

A Census Of Malton's Dublin				
DOGS	LADIES	HORSES	GENTLEMEN	CHILDREN
33	59	89	262	28

CHARLEMONT-HOUSE, DUBLIN.

London, Pub.d by Ja.s Malton & G. Cowen, Dublin June 1795.

21. Powerscourt House

MALTON INVITES US to look through the prism of the 1790s, but it is a fair challenge to situate oneself in the historical moment, with fresh eyes, looking forwards rather than backwards. We struggle to imagine Viscount Powerscourt – his country estate was in Enniskerry – asking Robert Mack to design a large townhouse in 1771. To modern eyes this is the view from Grogan's, the fine old pub on South William Street.

The property on view took three years to complete at a cost of £80,000. Malton calls it the third-finest house in the city: a 'pleasing, elegant structure'. Yet this townhouse was old-fashioned by the time it was completed. Its interior features two historical styles: the hallway and landing were decorated in a rococo style, while the ceiling in the music room and the ballroom are in a neoclassical style. The exterior is much the same today. Late at night, young people still smooch on those steps.

Powerscourt House is now a shopping centre, but in the last century it housed a draper's called Ferrier Pollocks. (The writer and poet Brendan Behan was once asked the difference between poetry and prose. He replied: 'There was a young lad called Rollocks, who worked in Ferrier Pollocks. One day on the Strand, with his girl in his hand, the water came up to his … knees. Now that's prose. But if the tide had been in, it would have been poetry.')

The street sign for Coppinger Row is in the same position today. To the right of it is an exhibition gallery – it was the first purpose-built exhibition space in these islands – that later became the Civic Museum. Today the building is occupied by the Irish Georgian Society.

Iconic streets lined with largely uniform brick townhouses, featuring beautiful doors framed by fanlights, give Georgian Dublin its character. Although the size of the houses varies, the style remains refined and tasteful, without much ornament or fuss. As the English writer V.S. Pritchett observed, 'The tall Georgian windows, the pilastered doorways, the fine fanlights, have a family dignity unspoiled by extravagance or pomp.'

POWERSCOURT-HOUSE, DUBLIN.

22. View from Capel Street, Looking Over Essex Bridge

THIS FAMILIAR ETCHING captures three key achievements of the Wide Streets Commission. We are looking from Capel Street over Essex Bridge (since replaced by Grattan Bridge) and up Parliament Street to the Royal Exchange, which is now called City Hall. We struggle to see this classic view with frank, unbloodied eyes.

Of all the views, this plate has the most street life. Malton – or one of his accomplices – peppers the streetscape with ladies, soldiers, urchins and kids. Look at the lads loitering, those creatures with baskets, the lamplighter, the barker, the hawker, those three dogs. But even this well-populated view is sanitized. For a start, where is all the horse manure?

Overcrowding reached a peak in Dublin towards the end of a century in which the population trebled. By 1791 most Dubliners lived not in Georgian mansions but in hovels. In the introduction to this book Diarmuid Ó Gráda writes of the poor souls who 'occupied the penumbra where it was hard to distinguish between the lowest jobs and mere reliance on charity'. The Dublin of *Juno and the Paycock*'s Joxer Daly has no place in the work of James Malton.

Malton pretends to give us Dublin from the inside, but this is an outsider's perspective. These views took the better part of ten years to publish as a single volume. This generous gift to Dublin was produced by an Englishman with a short-term interest in its success. His was a losing bet. As Andrew and Charlotte Bonar Law wrote, 'The production of the book caused him nothing but trouble, and it almost certainly lost him money.'

By the end of the century Malton must have known that he would never make it as an architect. So he found another subject. In 1800 he wrote a geometry manual, *The Young Painter's Maulstick*, and in 1802 he published *A collection of designs for rural retreats, as villas*. In the last act of his short life, an interest in British cottage architecture saw James Malton become a pioneer of the orné style. He never stopped trying.

Note the ship at anchor. Beyond its masts you can see the Old Custom House by Thomas Burgh (the architect of Trinity College Library), which was built in 1707 and remained in use until the new Custom House opened in 1791. Today this space is occupied by the Clarence Hotel.

VIEW FROM CAPEL-STREET, LOOKING OVER ESSEX-BRIDGE _ DUBLIN.

23. St Stephen's Green

THE GREEN WAS once a marshy common on the edge of town, used only for grazing and the odd execution. In 1664 Dublin Corporation decided to raise some revenue by sectioning off the park and selling off the surrounding land to speculators. Dubliners quickly embraced this verdant idyll, and since then it has mostly been a sanctuary in the heart of the city. But in 1937 the bronze statue of George II in the centre of the Green was blown up by the IRA. It is still missing a centrepiece.

For many years the most fashionable thing to do in Dublin was to parade up and down the north side of the Green. In this plate, perhaps the most charming of all the views despite the lack of an architectural focus, Malton captures the giddiness of the Beaux Walk, which was rather like a marriage market. Tinder for the eighteenth century. Look at the gentlemen puffing out their chests. This is a luxuriant portrait; there is sincere admiration as well as cheap flattery.

In 1792 the perimeter wall was breached by local gurriers. Plans were made to upgrade the Green, but these were abandoned to protect the Lord Mayor's grazing rights, a valuable perk. In the 1870s Arthur Edward Guinness loudly championed the opening of St Stephen's Green to the people of Dublin. He did not attend the official opening in 1880, but apparently spoke for forty-five minutes at the unveiling of a statue of himself. Lord Ardilaun is now remembered as a secular saint. Most visitors to this handsome park are unaware that in 1869 its patron was barred from the House of Commons because of a corruption scandal.

The first person commemorated in the Green was George II. His statue was erected in 1758; you can see it in the centre of this plate. The presence of the monarch politicized the space, and later there were calls to replace George with the Dublin-born Duke of Wellington. But a king could not be removed to make way for a subject.

St. STEPHEN'S GREEN, DUBLIN.

London Pub.d June 1796 by J. Malton

24. The Barracks

THE ROYAL BARRACKS were once among the largest in these islands. Built in 1706, they would eventually house 1,500 men and stables for cavalry, becoming the oldest continuously occupied barracks in Europe. After the Rebellion of 1798, Wolfe Tone was court-martialled and imprisoned here. City tradition has it that dozens of executed rebels were interred in the open ground lying between the Royal Barracks and the river, shown here as a pleasant pastoral space. The whole of Ireland would soon be punished for Emmet's apparent treachery with the loss of Dublin's parliament. As far as we know, James Malton never returned to the city that he worked so hard to promote.

On 28 July 1803 Malton died from 'a brain fever' at his home in Portland Place, London. He was thirty-eight years old. An obituary of this 'ingenious and distinguished artist' was published in *The Gentleman's Magazine*, but his death was not recorded in the Irish press. We don't know if he wrote the text ascribed to him in the Views. Yet this opaque figure, who died unmarried and childless, is now part of the tourist trail, and if we look closely at the pictures, they remind us that the Irish capital once had a golden age. But over-familiarity has blinded most of us to the man and the work.

Meet me in the Malton sunshine. (As the famous folk song 'The Dublin Saunter' has it, 'Dublin can be heaven with coffee at eleven and a stroll in Stephen's Green.') But that is to ignore the scale of his achievement, for this is the young man who gave future generations a lovingly crafted portrait of the city at the very moment of its self-realization. Malton's project highlights how the city was connected to a world of commerce, trade and artistic innovation, while also showing how these could be choreographed into an idea – even an ideal – of a city and society.

When Ireland secured its independence, the Royal Barracks were renamed Collins Barracks, and now they are home to the National Museum of Ireland. The museum owns several sets of Malton's prints, and over the years he has been the subject of major exhibitions. How poignant that the artist did not live to enjoy his fame.

BARRACKS, DUBLIN.

London, Published July 1795 by Ja.^s Malton.

25. View of Dublin from the Magazine Fort

This is the famous, much-copied view of Dublin from the Magazine Fort – where ammunition was stored – in the Phoenix Park. As usual, Malton gives us a sky sprinkled with clouds. Two young bucks survey the city. In the distance, you can just make out Islandbridge, then a new addition to the skyline. You can also see the Royal Hospital and the spires and domes of St Patrick's Cathedral and the Four Courts.

Good timing is part of the genius of this series. Desmond Guinness wrote that after the Act of Union, 'the Silver Lining crossed to England, leaving a dark cloud hanging over the city, which burst into flaming rebellion a hundred years later'. Long preserved by a cocoon of poverty, Georgian Dublin was left to rot and fall down for many years after the Irish secured independence. Today, an Irish patriot recognizes the cultural and aesthetic value of Georgian architecture.

Perhaps it is time for all of us to reconsider James Malton, the unsuccessful English draughtsman who gave us an aspirational idea of Dublin. He is still up there; still looking down from the walls of Dublin, even if we take him for granted; and at their best, his twenty-five etchings are an incitement to civic pride.

Another challenge is to rediscover the provocateur behind this over-ripe tribute, for in toasting Dublin at the height of its fame, the elusive artist dares us to do one better. Indeed, as we survey Dublin from the Magazine Fort in the Phoenix Park, let us honour James Malton by creating something more elegant and more thoughtful than just an ordinary city.

The Fort was built on a man-made hill in 1735; the idea was to protect the city, even though many Dubliners were destitute at that point. Jonathan Swift (pictured above) wrote of its construction:

> *'Behold! a proof of Irish sense!*
> *Here Irish wit is seen!*
> *When nothing's left, that's worth defence*
> *We build a Magazine.'*

VIEW of DUBLIN, from the MAGAZINE, PHOENIX-PARK.

London, Publish'd July 1796 by Jas. Malton.

Malton's Key to Plates 24 & 25

1. St Werburgh's Church
2. St Nicholas's Church
3. St Michael's Church
4. Christ Church Cathedral
5. St John's Church, John St
6. Steeven's Hospital
7. St Catherine's Church
8. Cupola of College Chapel
9. Dome of Four Courts
10. Arran Quay
11. Bloody Bridge
12. St Michan's Church
13. Cupola of Custom House
14. St Mary's Church
15. Royal Salute Battery
16. Steeple of Bluecoat Hospital
17. Royal Infirmary
18. St. Patrick's Church
19. Wood of East entrance to Kilmainham Hospital
20. Deputy Master's House of Hospital
21. Kilmainham Hospital
22. Avenue of West entrance to Hospital
23. Conduit for water
24. Mr. Harpur's Bleach-house
25. Mr. Gardner's Flourmill
26. Mr. Mander's Flourmill
27. Alderman Worthington's House
28. Sarah Bridge, once Island Bridge
29. River Liffey
30. Long Meadows
0. Houses on the Circular Road

A. Horse Barracks
B. Royal Square Foot Barracks
C. Small Square
D. Palatine Square
E. Riding House
F. Water Conduit
G. River Liffey
a. Houses on this side Barrack Street

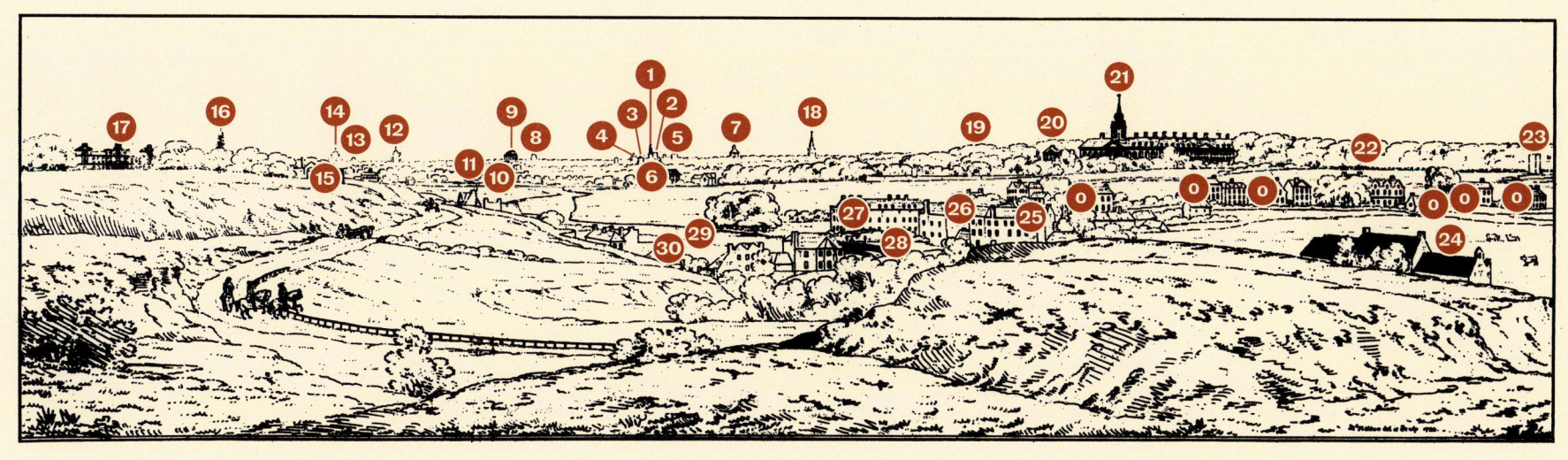
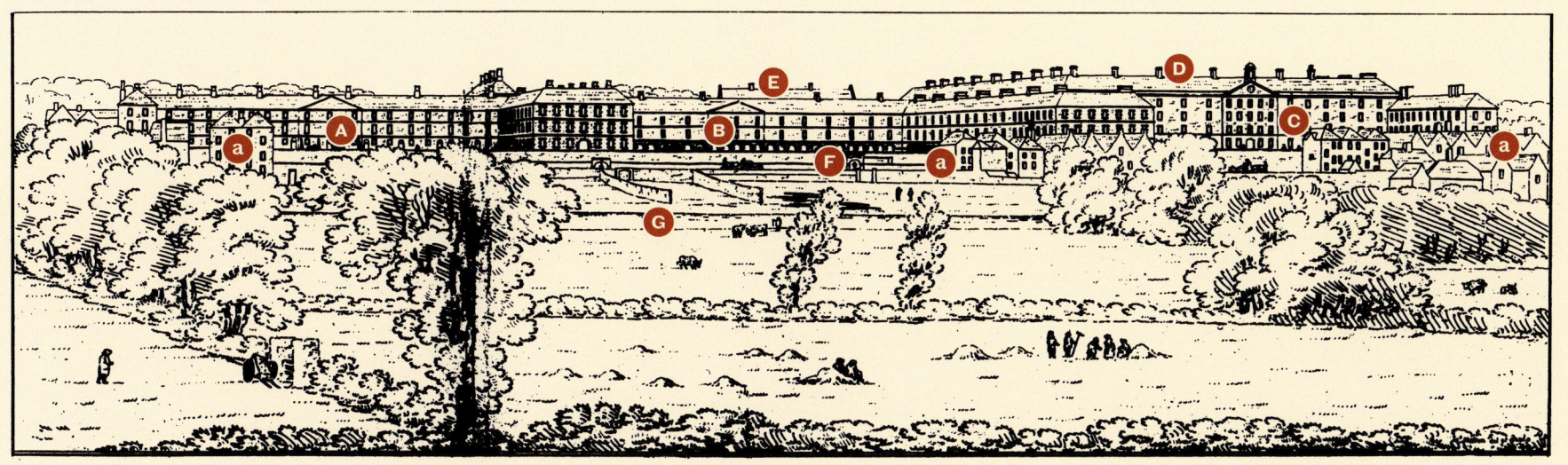

Best of Times, Worst of Times

DAVID DICKSON

James Malton's twenty-five engravings of Dublin were first published in London between 1792 and 1797, appearing at intervals in batches. The young Malton had been trained as an architectural draughtsman, coming to Dublin in the early 1780s to work for James Gandon (or so we are led to believe). Certainly the artist knew the city very well by the time he embarked on his great project: a series of views of Dublin, celebrating its architectural transformation. He did the necessary fieldwork in the course of 1791, choosing sites and making the set of original drawings on which his work would be based. These drawings, which he brought back to London, do not survive, but from them he produced both a number of luminous watercolours and his series of remarkable aquatints, the quality of which owes not a little to the fact that Malton carried out the engraving process himself. We can assume that much of the topographical detailing and finely proportioned representation of buildings and streetscapes were already there in his drawings, reflecting both his architectural training and his close encounters with Gandon's patrons, builders and presumably Gandon himself.

The engravings were published as a complete set in a single volume in 1799. However, the city that he had drawn so carefully in 1791 was a very different place by then. The start of the 1790s had been a time of great political excitement, with revolutionary turmoil in France promising to stir up dramatic changes at home. The general election in 1790 was particularly hard fought in the city, and the victorious popular candidates for the constituency, Lord Henry FitzGerald, heir to Leinster House (View 19), and Henry Grattan, the great parliamentary orator, had been paraded through town sporting French fashions and promising radical reform to their thousands of disenfranchised supporters. The political establishment was not so easily moved, but a sense that history was on the side of the reformers gave an infectious optimism to political debate in the guildhalls

Leinster House

and in the opposition newspapers. Even Dublin's great radical club, the Society of United Irishmen, which met first in the autumn of 1791, was a self-confident and outward-looking forum, embracing a version of the future where religious difference would carry no political weight.

The first years of the 1790s were also a time when the standard of living for most sections of Dublin society was improving. This was certainly the case for upper-class and bourgeois households: for property-owners, rental income from the countryside was rising; for merchants and professionals, demand from outside town for expensive goods and services was reaching unprecedented levels. Cross-channel exports were booming and wholesale markets thriving. The standard of living for skilled wage-earners, retailers and those in the construction trades was also rising, if less emphatically. The striking number of private and public building projects, particularly on the eastern side of the city, gave ample employment to the many unskilled earth-movers, stone-cutters, brickmakers and carters. Poverty was of course still present, to be found in the lanes, back yards and side streets in the western half of the city, but even for those living in poor housing and coping with bad sanitation, employment in the textile trades, food processing and retailing was greater than for many years past, and women and children were now being recruited into the new-style manufacturing enterprises in the suburbs.

Malton's images of Dublin in 1791 convey something of this economic buoyancy, with signs of a busy port (18), a spectacular new Custom House (9), and clean street scenes generating, in Maurice Craig's words, 'an atmosphere of Arcadian clarity'. Some of his thoroughfares seem abnormally quiet (e.g. 16), while others are shown with very light traffic and a few unhurried pedestrians – as in College Green (2, 3), Cross Poddle (7), Skinners Row/High Street (11), James Street (17), and South William Sttreet (21). Only the intersection at Capel Street/Essex bridge (22) seems moderately busy. Perhaps he did his fieldwork early in the morning or at other quiet times. Granted that with an armed metropolitan police force, established in 1786 and now fully active, the streets and street markets were more orderly than before, but they were likely to have been far busier than is suggested here. However, there was an artistic rationale: Malton's underpopulated streets allowed him draw the eye to the great public buildings. One of the most striking of these is his view of the Royal Exchange (8), a neoclassical masterpiece that predated both Gandon's and Malton's arrival in the city. Here there is plenty of distant coach and foot traffic to be seen along Dame

View from Capel Street [detail]

West front of St Patrick's Cathedral [detail]

The Upper Castle Yard
[detail]

Street, but in his treatment of the Exchange itself only a small group encroaches at the very corner of the building. Thus for busier – or more Hogarthian – representations of Dublin street life, one has to turn to Malton's contemporary John Nixon, although Nixon's work attracted little contemporary interest.

It was in the winter of 1792–3 that things began to go bad – the coming of the Anglo-French war, the first taste of political repression, a sharp credit crisis and a chill in the urban property market. Real wages were falling with higher food and alcohol prices, and a new malt tax in 1794 was deeply felt – and resented.

However, for several years the wider economy adapted to the war. Merrion Square was being completed, and large-scale speculative building on the eastern side of the Gardiner estate continued. In 1796 the Grand Canal was finally connected to the Liffey with the opening of the vast Grand Canal Docks.

But by then there was a growing chasm between the Irish government – based in the Castle (1) – and the prevailing political sentiment in the city outside, tinged by sectarian tensions, and this created an increasingly tense atmosphere. The French armada that briefly appeared out of the mists in Bantry Bay at the end of 1796, only to

The Barracks
[detail]

disappear again, was profoundly shocking to property-owners and the Irish government, and their reaction further polarized politics and public life. The property market shuddered to a halt and artisanal unemployment soared in the wake of the credit crisis of spring 1797. A now militant and subversive United Irish movement was organized in Dublin, and this led to censorship and eventually to martial law. Newgate prison on Green Street, one the largest public buildings not included by Malton, now housed hundreds of detainees. The great rebellion of May 1798 failed in Dublin, although it had been planned and orchestrated to a large extent by city radicals (including of course Lord Henry's young brother, Lord Edward FitzGerald), and this in turn led to bitter reprisals. City tradition has it that dozens of executed rebels were interred in the open ground lying between the Royal Barracks and the river, shown here as a pleasant pastoral space (24), but this remains unproven.

The 1798 rebellion set in motion plans in London for a dissolution of the Irish parliament and Anglo-Irish union. Malton's *Picturesque and Descriptive Views of Dublin* with its twenty-five engravings and accompanying text appeared midway through the bitter political battle over whether the parliament (2) would

The Lying-In Hospital
[detail]

vote itself out of existence. His text celebrated a capital city that had regularly brought several hundred wealthy families to reside in style during every parliamentary session. Opponents of the union predicted the closure of parliament would bring an aristocratic exodus, urban dereliction and industrial decay.

Dublin was indeed altered by the working out of the union, but the impact of the measure was not as predicted. With the survival, indeed growth, of central government institutions within the city during the early 1800s, public building projects continued and multiplied, and the great terraces of brick expanded outwards, particularly in the south-east quarter. The university blossomed and monumental welfare institutions proliferated, although none would ever match the neoclassical elegance of the Lying-In Hospital and Rotunda, featuring twice in Malton's views (15 and 16). But the Rotunda had been an essentially upper-class project, overseen by 'the men of taste' and the resident nobility. After Malton's time it was to be the State and the Churches which became the near-exclusive patrons of great building projects. Strangely no one followed in his steps to celebrate these, the great buildings of nineteenth-century Dublin. ❧

Picking through the details of James Malton's Dublin

Graham Hickey

On the surface, James Malton's Dublin is a carefully tailored series of vignettes that presents the Irish capital embellished with the essential tropes of eighteenth-century European urbanism. Neoclassical edifices dominate the collection, many of the first rank of public architecture. Riverine scenes bristle with marine activity, hinting at prosperity and global connections. Presentable streets, public spaces and institutions evoke a comforting gentility comparable to contemporary depictions of western cities. Only the occasional portrayal of bedraggled denizens hints at the vast seam of poverty that underpinned eighteenth-century Dublin society.

So ubiquitous are these images to the modern viewer, jaded by reproduction on table mats and prints lining the walls of hotel corridors, that they can be easily dismissed as nostalgic postcards of a romanticized past. Drill deeper, however, and a pin-sharp insight into the buildings, streetscape elements and social customs of Georgian Dublin can be gleaned. While much has not survived, many of Malton's depictions make sense of the fragmentary elements that have, and are important reference points for analysis.

For example, the changes made to buildings since their depiction in the 1790s present us today with options for restoration. Likewise, commonplace features and decorative conventions in Malton's views give us clues to a more sympathetic presentation of our historic buildings and streets. Even at elementary level, depictions of Georgian road surfaces and pavements, crafted from local, natural materials, direct us to a more sustainable and beautiful public realm. In short, Malton presents us with a direct line to the essential form of the eighteenth-century city that should be used as a springboard to preserve and enhance the character of Dublin's historic core in our own time. The extracts of his views reproduced here allow us to appreciate and better understand our urban inheritance through inspecting Malton's legacy at first hand.

If there is a uniting theme in Malton's perspectives of Dublin, it is the striking consistency of materials from which the city is hewn. Brick and stone provide a gratifying hierarchy in streetscape in a way Dubliners

Royal Exchange

largely take for granted compared to the mono-materiality of similar eighteenth-century cities such as Bath and Edinburgh. There, public buildings – civic, commercial, religious – must take their place amongst equally dressy stone-built domestic terraces, their primary trump card confined to an aggrandizement of scale and enrichment. In Dublin, the formula of stone-faced public buildings offset by reticent terraces built of red and yellow brick provides a much easier narrative and an instant legibility that inflects the heart of Malton's aesthetic.

His view of the Royal Exchange looking eastwards along Dame Street captures the gleaming Portland stone facades of architect Thomas Cooley's masterpiece, their brilliance heightened by a red-brick terrace to the east, newly erected under the auspices of the Wide Streets Commission. The same effect can be seen with Lord Powerscourt's mansion on South William Street, arguably one of the most successful compositions of the series. The mansion's rustic classical facade – *retardataire* for its time but immensely satisfying as street architecture – is lent a nobility by the genuflections of flanking red-brick houses and the brick-faced gallery of the Society of Artists. The view of the Rotunda Hospital from the west manages to create a palace of the 'Lying-In', flanked by the formal enclosure of red-brick houses on Cavendish Row, an effect repeated with Lord Charlemont's mansion further up Parnell Square – then Rutland Square – on the appropriately titled Palace Row. Even older, less fashionable streets sustain this metropolitan branding: the Tholsel on Skinner's Row, soon to be demolished after Malton's important record-taking, is lent a civic dignity – cumbersome columns and all – by the foil of undecorated brick houses. Further west, on Thomas Street, St Catherine's Church sits stoically, almost marooned, about the brick vernacular of the ancient highway to the agricultural hinterland. It is an urban structure that neatly lends itself to artistic representation, where public buildings are elevated as objects of desire and approbation amongst the premises of the everyman.

The downside is that depicting street buildings as primary subjects was not a priority for Malton, especially in secondary locations where older houses lingered. The ancient buildings of Thomas Street with their pointed and curvilinear gables, dormer roofs and fragments of timber-caged structures must have provided a picturesque urban scene, but Malton tells us little. Indeed, he is notably sketchy on the rambling vista of James's Street in the distant background of St Catherine's Church; its ranks of houses and the illusive agglomeration of buildings that comprised St James's

The Tholsel

St Catherine's Church

West front of St Patrick's Cathedral [detail]

Gate are tidily cast into shadow. His depiction of the north-western stretch of Dame Street, untouched by the Wide Streets Commission, is just as hazy, while the Liberties area – even with its churches, preaching halls and medieval remnants – goes entirely unrecorded.

Some tantalizing glimpses of the early Georgian city do slip through, such as the ranks of 'Dutch Billy' gable-fronted houses nestled next to St Patrick's Cathedral (as well as an early pan-tiled roof in the foreground). They are joined by gabled relatives dating to the 1720s on Sir John Rogerson's Quay and formerly gable-fronted houses on Skinner's Row next to the Tholsel, limply disguised with parapets – all of which record the prevalence of this distinctive typology that dominated the house building tradition in Dublin for over half a century from the 1690s. By contrast, Malton's view of Dublin from the Magazine Fort appears to deliberately capture a cluster of early buildings at Islandbridge, suggesting a tolerance for antiquity in picturesque environs over the grand parades of the metropolis.

Early fragments may also be seen in the evolution of window design charted by Malton. Exposed and flush sash-box frames, commonplace in the first half of the eighteenth century, can be seen creeping into the fringes of perspectives such as the tavern on the corner of St Catherine's Lane on Thomas Street (in addition to an antiquated dogtooth cornice at eave level) and on a shop-house flanking the Tholsel. Indeed, the Tholsel's fenestration is, itself, captured in an awkward state of transition, with original 1680s mullioned windows on the right-hand side and newer sashes to the left and centre – the latter's nine-over-nine pane formation an indication of the building's impressive scale.

Less apparent in the views are the dimensions of sash frames and glazing bars, which by Malton's time varied from the chunky *ovolo* proportions of the early 1700s to those described by Mrs Delany in 1759 – 'new made in the narrow way, which makes them much pleasanter' – turning slimmer still by the 1790s. 'Stone' was the shade predominantly favoured for windows at that time, an off-white generated by the murky tone of linseed oil then used to manufacture paint, as Malton's brightly depicted astragals testify.

One of the most illuminating details of Malton's views is the infrastructure used to light the city after dark. Until the early years of the nineteenth century, oil-fuelled lighting was the dominant technology prior to the adoption of gas lighting in 1825. Many of Malton's scenes give us a clear insight into these oil lamps, sadly not a single one of which still survives in its original form. Interestingly, it appears that regardless of public or private ownership, these lamps rarely deviated from a standard design. This consisted of a hand-spun glass globe suspended in a wrought-iron hoop, probably perched on a band of leather to avoid friction. A tin hat with a tapered chimney would fit snugly over the globe, inside which a small tray was suspended on wires, which held a puddle of oil and a wick. These would be filled and lit manually every day by a team of lamplighters, with the flame naturally extinguishing once the oil was exhausted.

Malton's view of Essex Bridge from Capel Street captures a lamplighter at work, in the late afternoon judging by the direction of the sunlight, precariously standing atop a ladder leaning against a lamp bracket, then often called a 'lamp iron'. This could take the form of a bracket projecting from a building, such as in his Grafton Street view, to upright standards mounted on railings like those shown on Rutland Square, to lamps tightly compressed against shopfronts – presumably to illuminate signage fascia boards.

Another form of metalwork in the form of lead downpipes can be identified in the views. Prior to the widespread adoption of cast-iron pipes c.1800, rainwater pipes were fashioned from rolls of lead and attached to facades with broad, clamp-like brackets, such as those

St Catherine's Church [detail]

The Tholsel [detail]

View from Capel Street [detail]

The Upper Castle Yard

visible on the far side of Essex Bridge and on the houses of Palace Row. Tellingly, the lower echelons of these pipes are often shown by Malton encased in boxing-out to protect them from impact and theft, especially apparent on the side elevation of the Bedford Tower in Dublin Castle.

The view of the Castle's Upper Yard may almost be a city in itself, bristling with chimneystacks and the ill-fated spire of St Werburgh's Church. The scene is enclosed with the bricked courtyard ranges designed by multiple Surveyors General, starting with William Robinson in 1684 and ending with Thomas Eyre in 1761. Malton's rendering is a vital record of the Castle's original Carolean dormered roof, a format primarily executed by Thomas Burgh in his substantial contribution to the courtyard's construction during the 1710s. By the 1790s the roofs were recorded as being notoriously leaky and were systematically replaced over the next forty years with a full additional storey – primarily by architect to the Board of Works Francis Johnston. We can also discern the original mid-1740s arrangement of the principal entrance to the State Apartments on the left, then an open loggia of Tuscan columns of Portland stone, prior to its enclosure with glazed timber screens in the early nineteenth century and subsequent partial rebuilding in the 1960s.

Malton also captures small details that change our perceptions of the eighteenth-century city. For example, chimney pots crown only about half of the chimneystacks depicted in his scenes – many remain open to the elements. Those pots that feature appear to be standard clay editions, while others suggest much chunkier affairs. Are these brick or even hollowed stone? Certainly sandstone was used as roof ridging in Dublin as late as the 1790s.

Brick as a building material is also a remarkably unifying theme in Malton's Dublin, much more so than in the modern city. Cement render and a multiplicity of crude interventions have since disfigured the satisfying totality of a brick city, where the front, side and rear elevations of buildings, their chimneys and ancillary structures all glowed in warm, textured unison. Malton's views hint at traditional brick techniques: wigging, gauged heads over windows, colour-washing and raddling.

The depiction of quaysides often devoid of walls and decorative balustrades also reminds us of the working nature of the river, central to Georgian Dublin's economy and its connection to the outside world. And shopfronts, designed to classical principles and displaying the wares of this trade, speak to contemporary visitors' favourable comparisons of Dublin fashion with other European cities.

There are curious omissions from the collection, such as Sackville Mall, then basking in a venerability and established aristocratic lineage. Had its opening to 'New' Sackville Street in the 1780s, extending the exclusive enclave to the Liffey, already tarnished its image by the time of Malton's drafting in 1791? The lower end of the thoroughfare and the new river crossing at Carlisle Bridge would also have been a hive of construction activity at the time. An internal view of Trinity College and Parliament Square is also absent, as are select views of the incomplete Merrion Square and the awkward hulk of Christ Church Cathedral.

If we are to take inspiration from Malton's record-keeping, it must surely be to restore the civic dignity and setting of our historic public buildings and spaces. It is dispiriting to observe how much of Malton's public realm has only recently been compromised by the heavy hand of the Luas Cross City project: unnecessarily slashing through College Green, creating an engineered monster of the setting of the Rotunda Hospital and Parnell Monument, and making a hostile canyon of the natural piazza outside the Provost's House. Some of his views are also destined to be irrevocably altered

Charlemont House [detail]

The Tholsel [detail]

The Rotunda & New Rooms

through the intrusion of ill-considered tall buildings: monuments to the greed of global finance and the vanity of indigenous developers that serve as its unconvincing local veneer.

But much can be enhanced with good placemaking. College Green can yet be grappled from motorized traffic and returned to the citizen as the capital's civic set-piece celebrated by Malton. Likewise, the future of the Rotunda complex is utterly integral to the cultural revival of the northside. The hospital's long-fingered decampment to a new location must be harnessed as a pivotal opportunity to create a cultural campus that intertwines its rich history of groundbreaking maternity services, philanthropy, leisure and the civic life of the city. The great Rotunda room, depicted by Malton newly dressed in Gandon-contrived 1780s neoclassical finery, should be the fulcrum of a restored entertainment complex, complete with public access to its eighteenth-century Assembly Rooms and restored Pleasure Gardens. Richard Castle's colonnaded set-piece and forecourt to the hospital, beautifully rendered by Malton but now mutilated and populated by car parking, must be carefully reconfigured and restored to its original state.

Small-scale stitching can have a transformative impact. Restoring Gandon's alternating niches on the river facade of the Custom House is an essential and easy win. Reinstating the missing classical urns atop the piers of the entrance screen of the Provost's House would lend theatre to this stretch of streetscape; likewise the missing baubles that Malton captures dressing the flank walls of the heroic entrance portals of Dublin Castle's Upper Yard. Authentic lamp irons demand a comeback on strategic streetscapes, buildings and squares, while traditional masonry skills could be advanced with Leinster granite and setted surfaces reinstated in key locations. Municipal incentives to reinstate sash windows and high-quality shopfronts would have similarly transformative effects on Dublin's streets. Above all, pushing private motorized traffic back to a semi-Georgian state of near oblivion is an essential step towards recolonizing the city with people, for people.

James Malton's Dublin is picture-postcard perfect. But this is not founded on nostalgia or selectivity alone. His scenography is alluring to us as true depictions of a working, living place that evolved through its inherent functionality. Its beauty, fine grain and humanity represent an epoch before the imposition of modern road-planning nonsense and hyper-globalized forces. It is a city where people lived, worked and entertained in largely the same place. Today, in an age of technology and boundless information, we would do well to take heed of the elegant townscapes of Malton's Dublin and learn from their elementary instruction. ❈

The Custom House [detail]

The Provost's House

Creating a Route to the Castle

Merlo Kelly

MALTON'S BUSTLING 'View from Capel-Street looking over Essex-Bridge, Dublin', captures a vibrant snapshot of life in the city at the close of the eighteenth century. This very particular view, south over the River Liffey from Capel Street, frames a section of the historic centre during a period of great transformation. The Wide Streets Commission, one of the first planning authorities in Europe, had been established in 1757 'for making a wide and convenient Way, Street, or Passage, from Essex-bridge to the Castle of Dublin'. A first task for the commission was the creation of a formal route between Capel Street and Dublin Castle, which led to the setting-out of Parliament Street in 1762. This development was one of a number of formative changes in the city, and signalled the beginning of a phase of enlightened urban planning.

James Butler, Duke of Ormonde, was influential in the consolidation of the Liffey quayside in the late seventeenth century, and this proved a critical step in shaping the city we recognize today. In 1680 developer Humphrey Jervis set out Ormond Quay on the lands of his estate, naming it after the Viceroy. Drawing influence from other European capitals, most notably Paris, generous boulevards were laid out along the river's edge, with red-brick terraces addressing the Liffey. Prior to this, the natural riverbank was lined with smaller dwellings, and lacked a formal structure. This transitional phase is nicely captured in Francis Place's 1698 drawing 'Dublin from the Wooden Bridge'.

'Dublin from the Wooden Bridge', Francis Place, 1698
(Image rights: National Gallery of Ireland)

Essex Bridge was built by Jervis in 1676, and stone from St Mary's Abbey was allegedly used in its construction. It was replaced in 1755 by what is now known as Grattan Bridge, or Capel Street Bridge. Capel Street formed the central spine in the gridded Jervis Estate, connecting the north city to Dame Street and the historic centre. The street was developed for residential use in the late seventeenth century, establishing an affluent neighbourhood to rival that of the Aungier Estate, south of the river. Many of the houses built along Capel Street at this time were gable-fronted 'Dutch Billys', later replaced by eighteenth-century Georgian townhouses, or adapted and enlarged.

Malton's view across Essex Bridge leads us down Parliament Street with the Royal Exchange (now City Hall) closing the vista. John Rocque's 1756 map of Dublin illustrates this new street configuration prior to the placement of Thomas Cooley's neoclassical Royal Exchange, which was completed in 1779. In Rocque's depiction, Bedford Square forms a public space at the castle entrance. The siting of the Royal Exchange along the prominent northern route to Dublin Castle, and close to the Custom House, reaffirmed the historic core as the commercial centre. This area immediately north of the castle was the established banking quarter at the time, with Thomas Ivory's elegant Newcomen Bank (1781) forming the corner to Castle Street and Cork Hill.

Malton offers a glimpse of the former Custom House, east of the bridge along Wellington Quay, then named Custom House Quay. Designed by Thomas Burgh in 1704, the steep roof pitch, dormers and substantial chimneys were typical features of this period. Illustrations accompanying Brooking's 1728 map of Dublin reveal this stretch of the quayside in greater detail. Alongside the Custom House, tall structures with narrow closet returns are set back from the riverfront, their rear elevations to the Liffey. This section of the city was later reconfigured with the development of Wellington Quay. In 1780 a decision was made to relocate the Custom House to its present position, on the newly formed quayside east of O'Connell Street (then Sackville Street). It was without doubt of strategic interest to many members of the Wide Streets Commission such as Gardiner and Fitzwilliam, who were developing their estates to the east. The proposal was steeped in controversy and met with strong resistance from the merchant population. There was such opposition to the move that the architect of the new Custom House, James Gandon, reputedly carried a sword when attending site visits!

Aside from the architectural insights it allows, Malton's street scene serves to document the diverse

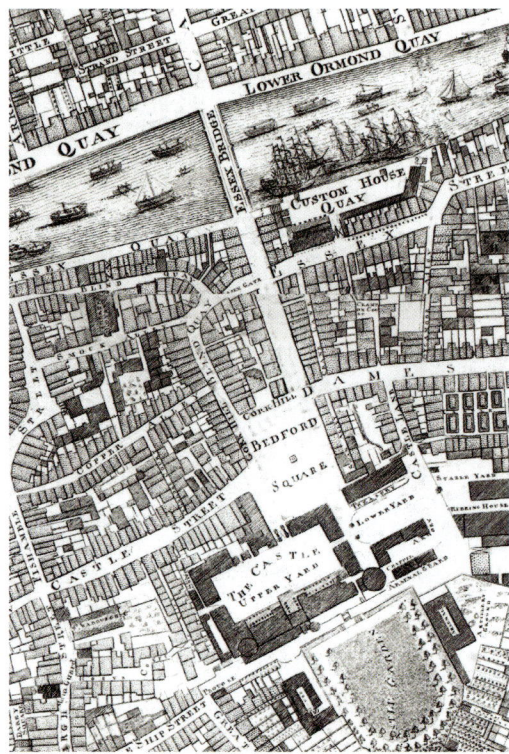

'An exact survey of the City and Suburbs of Dublin', John Rocque, 1756 [detail]
(Image rights: Irish Historic Towns Atlas / Royal Irish Academy)

'A map of the City and Suburbs of Dublin', Charles Brooking, 1728 [detail] (Image rights: Irish Historic Towns Atlas / Royal Irish Academy)

social landscape in the city at the time, presenting a neat cross-section of eighteenth-century society. Elegantly dressed women are pictured alongside impoverished figures begging, and street dogs. A labourer pushes his wheelbarrow across the bridge, where the lamplighter scales a ladder to illuminate the street lights. Burgh's nearby Royal Barracks (1707) may explain the presence of the mounted soldiers parading the quayside. The masts of an impressive trading ship are visible over the quay walls. It should be noted that following the strategic placement of Carlisle Bridge in 1795 (later replaced and renamed O'Connell Bridge), large ships could no longer access this stretch of the Liffey. This further compounded the move eastwards from the historic mercantile centre.

Perhaps most interestingly, the lively scene captures a turning point on Capel Street, when it evolved from a residential street to one lined with shops and businesses. The Wide Streets Commission had introduced the notion of 'Living over the shop' in their proposals for Cavendish Row in 1787, drawing influence from emerging European trends and house typologies. Upper levels housed the living quarters and were typically accessed independently of the shop below. These new living arrangements reflected a societal shift, and the emergence of a rising 'middle class'. As the demand for commercial property grew, many townhouses were adapted to accommodate shop premises at street level. Capel Street echoed this trend and, by the early nineteenth century, the area had become a thriving commercial hub. Malton's print depicts the newly established decorative timber shopfronts and ornate windows which came to line the street, enhancing the plain brick facades.

A City of Rare Habits: James Malton's Dublin

KATHRYN MILLIGAN

WRITING ABOUT James Malton's view of Powerscourt House (21), Eavan Boland described eighteenth-century Dublin as 'a city with huge wings, / a city of rare habits'; eloquently capturing the breath and energy of that period in the city's history.[1] While the chief interest of Malton's view is the large mansion at the centre of the composition, much can be gleaned about eighteenth-century consumer life from the details he included in the margins. On the right-hand side of the image, we see two men converse outside the City Assembly Rooms. The figure on the steps appears to be emerging from the building, pulling on his gloves as he does so, while his companion rests easily on horseback. The latter man's outstretched arm draws the viewer's attention to the window behind him: something has also caught the eye of the one of silk- and lace-clad ladies walking on the street. Here, in a detail that might be easily overlooked, we enter the commercial world of the eighteenth-century city. Adorning the centre of the 'Fruit Warehouse' window display is a large pineapple, surrounded by smaller, unfortunately indistinguishable, fruits or flowers. Described by Malton as 'a confined, but genteel, private street', this detail also suggests that it is a fashionable one, sustained by a market for luxury goods brought into the city to supply the best tables.

James Malton (1765–1803) was born into a family of London-based architectural draughtsmen and publishers. His father, Thomas Malton (1726–1801) was a cabinet-maker turned draughtsman, who published two books on geometry and perspective, the second of which garnered significant Irish patronage through subscriptions. Although beset by financial difficulties and uneven support from his patrons, Malton senior established a link between the family and the Irish city, furthered through their acquaintance with the architect

---

1 Eavan Boland, 'On Seeing James Malton's Powerscourt-House, Dublin 1795', *The Stinging Fly* 6, 2 (2007): 10.

James Gandon (1743–1823). James's brother, Thomas Malton Jnr (1752–1804) also worked as an architectural draughtsman and may have had some training from Gandon in the late 1770s. As will be seen, the outputs of Thomas and James are closely linked, particularly their pursuit of elite patronage through publication. James Malton, then, was initially trained in the family business by his father, and from 1781 he was employed by Gandon as a drawing clerk in Dublin. Aged in his late teens, Malton did not complete his five-year term with the architect, and after a short period in London, he returned to Dublin for seven more years. During this time, from 1785 to 1792, Malton completed the preparatory sketches for his best-known pictorial work: *A Picturesque and Descriptive View of the City of Dublin*, published initially in series of folios from around 1792 and later as a single volume of twenty-five views.

Malton's book of Dublin views contributed to a then-burgeoning market for large-format illustrated travel books, made for well-to-do patrons, subscribers and purchasers. Advances in print technology in the latter half of the eighteenth century facilitated this growth, not least through the popularization of aquatint, or as Malton and his contemporaries referred to it, 'aquatinta'. Previous publications on the history of Dublin, such as Robert Pool and James Cash's *Views of the Most Remarkable Public Buildings, Monuments and other Edifices in the City of Dublin* (1780) or other near contemporary texts (like John Ferrar's *A View of Ancient and Modern Dublin*, published in 1807) relied on less sophisticated engravings of the city's architecture, clearly lacking the artistic sensibility sought and promoted by Malton. In Britain, an acquaintance of the Malton family was a key pioneer in this new medium: Paul Sandby (1731–1809) had trained as a military draughtsman and landscape painter, travelling with the army to various locations, including Dublin. During the 1770s Sandby began to experiment with aquatint: this new method enabled the artist to capture the tonal and wash effects of watercolour in print, creating a more painterly and textured effect than engraving alone. Sandby found that the process was particularly adept for capturing landscape scenes: some of his earliest experiments in the medium showed the Welsh countryside and coast. The aquatint could be further enhanced through the application of thin washes of watercolour, a process known as hand colouring, completed either by the artist, printer, or by a third party. As Douglas Fordham has outlined, from its inception, the aquatint process was aligned to topographical draughtsmanship (and its military uses), the production of folios or books, and the nebulous aesthetic category of the picturesque. Commented on extensively by eighteenth-century aesthetes (most notably William Gilpin), the 'picturesque' encompasses a subject (usually a landscape), how it is presented, and the effect it has on the viewer: the focus was at once on 'scopic pleasure', the visual framing of the subject and its legibility, as well as the elision or reduction of difficult social realities.[2] When combined, the process of aquatint, theories of the picturesque, and the book trade, created a 'set of material practices', which established 'new modes of seeing and representing the world': through an illustrated publication, where aquatint images were joined by a letterpress description, readers could experience the world without leaving the comfort of their own homes.[3]

This visual and commercial history is important for understanding the audience that Malton sought to reach with his Dublin views. Furthermore, it was an audience that his brother, Thomas Malton Jnr, was also trying to capture with his own series of aquatint prints, the first part of which was published in 1792, and completed in 1801. Showing the architecture, streets, and other sites of the City of London and Westminster, Thomas's series was undoubtedly more ambitious than his younger brother's Dublin series: it ultimately totalled one hundred plates and was sold in two volumes at a cost of £14 4s. each. As the list of subscribers shows, Thomas's venture was supported by a cross-section of artistic and society patrons. Although there is no corresponding list for the Dublin volume, Malton would surely have sought to capitalize on the social world of connections, flattery and imitation: indeed, this is evident through the dedications to notable figures in the letterpress descriptions of each plate. Conceived of and published in the decade prior to the Act of Union, and still being actively advertised in its aftermath, many of those to which Malton sought to pay court were navigating a new relationship with the Irish city. However, patronage from these elite circles was necessary: complementing the world of commerce and consumption portrayed in its pages, *A Picturesque and Descriptive View* was itself a luxury product. As a bound folio of twenty-five prints, the prices for a copy ranged from £6 16s. 6d. 'in boards'; £7 7s. 6d. 'elegantly bound'; and £8 8s. for an edition 'elegantly bound, with a portfolio or extra cover'. The luxurious nature of the volume was also reflected in its size: the bound folio was produced in 'imperial size' meaning that the volume would need to be placed on a flat surface (with support for the binding) to be perused by the viewer. Sold through fashionable stationers and print-sellers in London and Dublin, the artist may have imagined his volume on an elegant table in a

2 Douglas Fordham, *Aquatint Worlds: Travel, Print, and Empire, 1770–1820* (London: Paul Mellon Centre for Studies in British Art, 2019), 35.

3 Ibid., 42.

morning room or library; prominently displayed for the enjoyment of visitors. These material elements of Malton's original series are easily lost in the subsequent reprintings and reformatting of his compositions through the eighteenth, nineteenth and twentieth centuries.

Returning to the view of Powerscourt House and South William Street (21), we can find in this image the bringing together of eighteenth-century luxury, commerce, and the picturesque through its architectural and social detail, including through the window display of the fruit shop. In the eighteenth century the pineapple was 'a highly desired colonial commodity', not only making its appearance in shop windows, and dining rooms, but reproduced as a 'fashionable decorative motif … on gateposts, samplers, wallpaper, tea services, fans, furniture, and even fabric'.[4] Pineapples appeared on tables across the country, and in some instances were even cultivated in Ireland.[5] The important chronicler of eighteenth-century Irish life, Mary Delany, recalled that in 1758 she had ten pineapples 'sent me from Dublin … as fine ones as ever I tasted, by Lord Charlemont's orders'.[6] The following year she also wrote to her sister that while

[4] Joanna M. Gohmann, 'Colonizing through Clay: A Case Study of the Pineapple in British Material Culture', *Eighteenth-Century Fiction* 31, no. 1 (2018): 143–4.

[5] See Toby Barnard, *Making the Grand Figure: Lives and Possessions in Ireland, 1641–1770* (New Haven and London: Yale University Press, 2004), 195.

[6] Mrs Delany to Mrs Dews, 9 September 1758, *The Autobiography and Correspondence of Mary Granville*, Mrs Delany, 511.

visiting 'Mrs Clement's Lodge in the Phoenix Park,' … 'a pineapple was brought in ready pared and cut, all served in fine old china'.[7] Comparison with these types of contemporary records shows how Malton's views of Dublin chimed with its material reality, even if only for its wealthier inhabitants. As Donough Cahill and David Fleming have noted, Malton altered elements of William Street for this print: the steps of the Assembly House have been extended across its facade; the basement and its attendant railings have been omitted; and the artist has significantly reduced the width of the opening to Coppinger's Row: the elegantly bowed shop window is also an amendment to what's seen there today.[8] These alterations are tangible evidence of how Malton moulded his view of Dublin to create a picturesque streetscape: allied to this, we can also consider how, through details like tropical fruit, silk clothing and fine carriages, he created a consumer landscape that aligned with what his patrons *wanted* to see, rather than a simple translation from street, to sketchbook, to copper plate and to print. Newspaper records suggest that for a short time in the 1790s, the perfumer and fruit merchant James Middlewood had premises at 57 William Street (the next building along to the City Assembly House) in addition to a larger wholesale and retail warehouse at 46 Fishamble Street. Could Malton have been inspired by this neighbouring shop when he set about his composition? Or, perhaps, being aware of the current fashion for the commodity, he may also have imagined the visual and material desires of the patron who would purchase his publication, and consciously courted this with the type of city he sought to present.

When viewed in the book- and print-sellers' shops of Dame Street, Pall Mall, Bond Street or Holborn, Malton's prints of Dublin were tasked with not only disseminating the history and notable architectural features of Dublin, but with impressing upon the reader or viewer its desirability as a fashionable centre of commerce and sociability. For those unfamiliar with the city, Malton's views offered a glimpse into a place outside of the everyday – chiming with a growing taste for imagery of new and interesting places within the parameters of the picturesque view. The importance of *A Picturesque and Descriptive View of the City of Dublin* to Dublin's eighteenth-century history transcends its value as a chronicle of its architectural features: through its subjects, both real and imagined, and its material form, it highlights how the city was connected to a world of commerce, trade and artistic innovation, while also showing how these could be choreographed into an idea, or even an ideal, of a city and society. ❦

7 Mrs Delany to Mrs Dewes, 22 September 1759, in *The Autobiography and Correspondence of Mary Granville, Mrs Delany; with interesting reminiscences of King George the Third and Queen Charlotte. Edited by the Right Honorable Lady Llanover, Volume III* (London: Richard Bentley, 1861), 582.

8 Donough Cahill and David Fleming, 'From the Society of Artists to the Irish Georgian Society: The City Assembly House and its uses, 1766–2018', in D. Fleming, R. Kenny, and W. Laffan (eds), *Exhibiting Art in Georgian Ireland: The Society of Artists' Exhibitions Recreated* (Dublin: Irish Georgian Society, 2018), 82.

Note on Contributors

DAVID DICKSON is Professor Emeritus of Modern History at Trinity College Dublin. His books include *Dublin: The Making of a Capital City* (2014) and *The First Irish Cities: An Eighteenth-Century Transformation* (2021).

GRAHAM HICKEY is Conservation Director at Dublin Civic Trust. He is author of *Meath & Francis Streets: A Study of the Past, A Vision for the Future* for Dublin Civic Trust, and a contributor to numerous built heritage policy documents.

MERLO KELLY is a Conservation Architect with Lotts Architecture & Urbanism and a Design Fellow at the School of Architecture, University College Dublin. Her research into James Hoban was published in *James Hoban: Designer and Builder of the White House* (2021).

KATHRYN MILLIGAN is a historian specializing in nineteenth- and twentieth-century Irish art. Her first monograph, *Painting Dublin, 1886–1949: Visualising a changing city* (2020) is published with Manchester University Press.

DIARMUID Ó GRÁDA is a planning consultant and lecturer in planning at University College Dublin. His book *Georgian Dublin: The Forces That Shaped the City* was published in 2015.

TREVOR WHITE is director of The Little Museum of Dublin. He was the founding publisher of *The Dubliner* magazine and is the author of four books.

Acknowledgements

This book stems from a publication produced in 2020 by The Little Museum of Dublin with the support of Tony Reddy and his colleagues in Reddy Architecture + Urbanism. Tony cares passionately about the city of Dublin and his support was crucial to the publication of the original work.

The Little Museum of Dublin is a registered charity governed by an unpaid Board of Directors: Miriam Brady, Ed Brophy, Councillor Deirdre Conroy, Catriona Crowe, Councillor Mary Freehill, Brian Geraghty, The Lord Mayor of Dublin, Susan McKeon, Dr Rhona Mahony, James Ryan and Brody Sweeney (chairman).

Special thanks to Andrew Bonar Law, Sarah Costigan, Michael Darcy, Antony Farrell, Edwin Higel, Niall McCormack, Stephen Reid, Mary Stanley, Susan Jane White; and to Adam's, Whyte's, The National Gallery of Ireland and The Lilliput Press for use of material.

The photographs of Malton's vantage points today were taken by Gintaras Varnagys. Michael Darcy wrote the keys to the maps.